Emil Reich

History of Civilization

Graeco-Roman institutions, from anti-evolutionist points of view; Roman

law, classical slavery, social conditions. Four lectures delivered before the

University of Oxford

Emil Reich

History of Civilization
*Graeco-Roman institutions, from anti-evolutionist points of view; Roman law,
classical slavery, social conditions. Four lectures delivered before the University of
Oxford*

ISBN/EAN: 9783337412067

Printed in Europe, USA, Canada, Australia, Japan

Cover: Foto ©ninafisch / pixelio.de

More available books at **www.hansebooks.com**

GRAECO - ROMAN INSTITUTIONS,

FROM ANTI - EVOLUTIONIST POINTS OF VIEW.

ROMAN LAW,
CLASSICAL SLAVERY,
SOCIAL CONDITIONS.

Four Lectures delivered before the University of Oxford,

BY

EMIL REICH, Doctor Juris,

AUTHOR OF "LECTURES ON THE HISTORY OF CIVILIZATION."

———————•———————

Parker and Co.

BROAD-STREET, OXFORD;

AND 6 SOUTHAMPTON-STREET, STRAND, LONDON.

1890.

————————

PREFACE.

By kind permission of the authorities of the University of Oxford, the following four lectures were delivered at "The Schools," on 7th, 14th, 21st February, and 7th March, 1890, respectively. In his endeavour to cover a series of vast problems within the limited space of four lectures the author was obliged to use very concise language, restricting himself to the leading features of his subject. This was all the more difficult since the views advanced deviate most essentially from many current views on the issues discussed, more particularly from the opinions regarding the rise and growth of the science of Roman Law, Graeco-Roman slavery, and the applicableness of modern evolutionist theories to the study of social institutions. Every line of the present lectures has the virtual or actual tendency to disprove the applicableness of Darwinian concepts to the solution of sociological problems. The author begs to introduce them as a brief *exposé* of a portion of his forthcoming work on the history of the main institutions of civilization. He also takes this opportunity to extend his best thanks to all the Professors, Fellows, Tutors, and Undergraduates of the University of Oxford who honoured him with their attendance.

EMIL REICH.

Paris, Bibliothèque Nationale,
25th April, 1890.

CONTENTS.

———◆———

Lectures on the History of Civilization.

GRAECO-ROMAN INSTITUTIONS.

I.

THE *VERA CAUSA* OF ROMAN LAW.

Romans not likely to create a science of Private Law.—In what con-
sists the specific perfection of Roman, as contrasted with English
and Mohammedan Law?—The causes of Roman Law were
neither religion (*Coulanges*), nor race-character and "Ideas"
(*Ihering*), nor "early codification" (*Maine*), nor "healthy
nationality" (*Mommsen*). Outlines of the *vera causa.*

THE most superficial glance at the development of
Western civilization cannot fail to notice that certain
nations succeeded in maturing some branches of art to
a degree of perfection unknown amongst other peoples.
Thus sculpture was brought to its highest pitch of perfection by the Greeks; painting by the Italians and
Spaniards; music by the Germans. Science, on the
other hand, seems, to use the words of Goethe, to be
a fugue, the successive parts of which are formed by the
contributions of *all* nations, and while some nations may
boast a greater number of meritorious scientists than
others, no nation of Western civilization so completely
excels its competitors in the domain of science, as do
some in the realm of art.

To this general remark there is one exception, and
one only: namely *Roman Law.*

Roman Law as taught in the writings of the Roman
jurists is a science, a science of great perfection, a science

so perfect as to almost approach the harmonious finish of art. But Roman Law is not only a marvellous system of the legal customs and concepts of the Romans; its value is not restricted to students of *Roman* Law; it has an absolute value for students of any law whatever. In other words, the Romans outstripped all other nations, both ancient and modern, in the scientific construction of legal problems. They alone offer that curious example of one nation's totally eclipsing the scientific achievements of all other nations.

By law, however, we here understand not all branches of law, as constitutional, criminal, pontifical, and private law, together with jurisprudence. By Roman Law we mean exclusively *Roman Private Law.* The writings of Roman jurists on constitutional and criminal law have been superseded and surpassed by the writings of more modern jurists. Their writings on questions of Private Law, on the other hand, occupy a unique place; they are, to the present day, considered as the inexhaustible fountainhead, and the inimitable pattern of the science of Private Law. This statement stands in need of no evidence; it is conceded on all hands. It stands, however, in need of an historical and technical explanation.

In other words, it is perfectly legitimate to ask, why were the Romans the only nation of Western civilization that could bring forth a scientific system of Private Law?

This question is all the more legitimate, because the Romans, of all nations, were the least likely to produce a scientific system of Private Law. Roman History down to Augustus had two main features : (1) the conquest of the world round the Mediterranean; (2) the internal strifes for constitutional rights and privileges, first between the patricians and plebeians, and afterwards between the oligarchical and democratical classes. Now the wars of the Romans could not have been the foster-earth of a science of Private Law. The continuous constitutional strifes were, by their very nature, not unfavourable to the rise of jurists, chiefly because the great orators and lawyers of Rome represented at once the journalistic and parliamentary powers of our days. Men like Porcius Cato, Hortensius, or Cicero, united in themselves the parliamentary power of a modern Gladstone, with the vast influence of a newspaper like *The Times.* They were talking "leaders." Hence discussions of constitutional questions were a matter of daily occurrence, and thus we could not feel astonished had the Roman jurists left us a perfect science of *constitutional* law.

This, however, is not the case. Their writings on constitutional law are immeasurably below their writings on private law. In fact, our astonishment at the Romans having been the greatest writers on the science of Private Law becomes intensified the more we think of it.

Private Law feeds on commercial and industrial relations: the Romans held commerce in contempt, as all military peoples do, and industrial enterprises were given over to slaves. The practice of Private Law goes with so many annoyances and inconveniences that nobody can be expected to devote much time to the carrying on of another man's law-suits, unless he is paid for it: the Romans, until very late, never paid fees to their jurists. The cultivation of a science is generally the work of a profession, whose members have gone through a regular course of general mental training, and, more particularly, with regard to their special science: the real founders of the science of Roman Law were unprofessional people who did not cultivate the science of law to the exclusion of all other avocations. Besides, the Romans never cultivated any science with great zeal or success. Science they took at second-hand from the Greeks. For the Greeks were *the* scientists of the world.

The cities that studded the shores of the Aegaean, Tyrrhenian, and Ionian seas poured forth ever-increasing numbers of profound thinkers, who contrived to marshal into scientific order facts of the most divergent descriptions. The disconnected experiences and observations of butchers, hunters, fishers, and bird-catchers they dexterously and most ingeniously welded into systematic views of comparative anatomy. The incoherent and stray glimpses of plant-life caught by the gardener, florist, and forester they collected into luminous views on botanical phenomena. The intricate and irregular verbal and syntactical phenomena of their marvellous idioms they succeeded in arranging according to comprehensive principles. And likewise with other phenomena, astronomical, mechanical, mathematical, and political. It is needless to enumerate the immortal names of Thales, Democritus, Pythagoras, Aristotle, Archimedes, Conon, Euclid, Theophrastus, Hipparchus, Heron, Diophantus, and all the other glories of Greek science.

Jurists, scientific jurists alone the Greeks never had. The Greeks construed sciences of all kinds of phenomena, legal phenomena of civil life excepted. Their wonderful gift for systematic thinking failed them in this one respect. Not even the laborious J. A. Fabricius could muster up more than a very small list of Greek jurists, in the Roman sense of the word, that is to say, jurists practising private law. Read the speeches of Isaeos or Isocrates, and compare their conception and treatment of law with similar passages in Cicero's Orations, for instance, the Oration for Caecina, or Quintius, or Murena, and the vast difference between Greek and Roman Private Law will strike you most forcibly.

In other words, the Greeks who were the teachers of the Romans in every branch of science and philosophy, were entirely unable to vie with their pupils as to legal science. Whence this remarkable and unexpected superiority of the Romans? How and why could they excel the most gifted nation of all ages in the cultivation of a science, the subject-matter of which was as familiar to the Greeks as to the Romans? For the Greeks were notorious pettifoggers, and there was scarcely a week but what a Greek took part in judicial proceedings, either as one of the numerous judges, or as a witness, or as one of the contending parties.

And why did the *Jews* not construct a *generally* valuable system of Private Law? They, as well as the ancient Egyptians, Assyrians, Icelanders, and Irish, had accumulated vast piles of legal casuistics, and the discussion of questions concerning Private Law, together with religious issues, formed the bulk of the studies eagerly pursued by Egyptian priests, Jewish rabbis, Irish "brehons," and Iceland wise men. Why, then, did they not succeed?

For make allowances as many as you may, the systems of Private Law, as cultivated among the nations just mentioned, are essentially inferior to the system taught in the writings of Roman jurists. You will ask, perhaps, in what then does this vaunted superiority consist? Are the Roman jurists so much more sagacious or shrewd than the jurists of other nations? Is their practical sense so much stronger, or do they combine theoretical comprehensiveness with practical adroitness in a superior way?

It would be simply unfair to deny the exquisite keenness and penetration in the juristical portions of the *Thalmud* of the Jews, made accessible through the labours of M. Rabbinovicz; the *Gragas* of the Icelanders; or the amazing casuistics of the Brehon books. Nor can we discover any

serious deficiency in their sense of practical needs. They
also abound in refined principles, in systematic divisions,
sub-divisions, and sub-sub-divisions. And yet all this is
productive of no result of *generally* available excellence.
We read the ancient Brehons, because we take great historical interest in Irish institutions. But we never so much
as think of grafting law-principles of the ancient Brehons
on the body of our modern law, nor do we apply to them
for ready counsel and advice in any practical difficulty
of the bar or the bench.

The Romans, on the other hand, stand to us in intimate relation ; their legal wisdom is a living wisdom, a
living factor in our life. Marcus Antistius Labeo, Capito,
Gaius, Papinianus, Paulus, or Ulpian, are still walking
amongst us, ready to help us in any practical difficulty,
and capable of assisting us whenever we fail to make up
the feud between theory and practice. The works of the
Greek scientists and thinkers, although indicative of an
incomparably greater power of mind than the works of the
Roman jurists, are now-a-days obsolete. We rarely or never
use them as text-books, or as current reference-books of
science. The works of the Roman jurists, on the other
hand, still continue to be the text-books of students of law
all over Europe and America. In what then does this
specific excellence consist?

/   It is of course extremely difficult to reduce the charac-
terization of a complex system of Law to a few words. But
such is the pre-eminent excellence of Roman Private Law
that it is more or less easily contrasted with the system
of Private Law of other nations. *Roman or Civil Law is
the only system of Private Law that has not been unduly
influenced by the irrelevant factors of Religion, Politics, and
Ethics.*

Take the Private Law of any other nation. Let us begin

with English Law. We all know that English Common
Law has been largely influenced by the political structure
of English society. The English Law of real property,
for instance, is, in the words of Mr. Kenelm Digby, its
distinguished historian, a " congeries of ancient custom and
mediæval and modern innovation." But what were those
ancient customs and mediæval innovations caused by?
By the *political* system of feudalism. The law of acquiring
or conveying property was strictly and immediately de-
pending on the political standing of the owner or pur-
chaser. The pervading principle of the law of real property, as it developed in England, was this: " *Nulle terre
sans seigneur ;*" that is to say, the law of real property was
pervaded by a *political* principle. Consequently the strictly
legal, or to apply an unusual but very apt expression, the
strictly " *civilistic*" development of the law of real property
was hampered and interfered with from the very beginning.
An element was brought into it, that was irrelevant, because extraneous.

The Romans never suffered their legal institutions to be
interlarded with extraneous matter. From the earliest
times down to the age of the Emperors, the Romans had
a political institution that might have lent itself very easily
to an undue interference with institutions of Private Law,
after the manner of feudalism. I mean the Roman *clientela.*
Roman clients stood to their *patroni* in a relation not
unlike that of a feudal tenant to his lord. They held
estates from them, they were obliged to do homage and
to discharge some of the duties implied in "feudal incidents." All this surely might have easily been used as
a means to unduly influence the development of the Roman
Law of real property. It might have been used to create
those semi-complete forms of property with which English
law abounds, and which go to make the English law

of real property a most intricate law. But nothing of the
kind happened. The Roman concept of real property, or
rather of property in general, was nowise influenced by the
grants of land so frequent amongst patrons and clients,
and the legal construction of these grants, namely the
precaria, exercised no influence whatever on the features
of *dominium* or *possessio.*

Or take another great political institution of the Romans :
I mean the two classes of *patricians* and *plebeians.* Nothing is more patent than the constant struggle of the plebeians with the patricians, and the marked difference
in their political standing. Did this well-known difference
exercise any influence on the private law of the Romans?
Do we ever hear of an *actio* or private right being denied
to a Roman because he is a plebeian? There is no trace
either in the XII. Tables, or in any later legislation of any
thoroughgoing or even important difference between the
plebeians and patricians as to " civil " rights (taking the
word "civil " in its Roman sense) after the middle of
the fifth century B.C. A plebeian could acquire real property, contract obligations, marry and will his property
according to the same principles of Private Law as a patri-
cian. Their contentions and conflicts referred to *political*
issues. It never occurred to them to alter the frame of
their Private Law on the strength of political differences.
Consequently Private Law had not to suffer from an irrelevant mixture of extraneous matter, and instead of being
warped, as it were, in its development by the alien element
of politics, it freely pursued its natural course, and thus
reached a higher perfection.

Roman Law was likewise free from an undue influence
of Religion. What vast changes may be wrought in the
character of Private Law by an undue influence of Religion, or rather Theology, we can clearly see in the Law

of the Mohammedans, or, more correctly speaking, in the systems of the various sects of the Mohammedans. There are three gigantic systems of Private Law: the Roman, the English, and the Mohammedan. Each of them rules several hundreds of millions of people. But one glance at the sources of Mohammedan Private Law will satisfy us as to the reason of its inferiority compared to Roman Law. The order of authorities to be observed by a Mohammedan judge is (1) the Kooran, (2) the Soonut, or Traditions, (3) the concurrent opinions of the Sahabah, or Comparison of the Prophet, (4) the concurrent opinion of the Tabieen, or their immediate successors, (5) opinion of Abu Huneefa, Aboo Yoosuf, and Mohammed, (6) opinion of modern lawyers, (7) Kiyas, or analogical reason[a]. This of course refers to judges applying the Law according to Aboo Huneefa. But this "sect," together with all other "sects," recognize the Kooran, the Sahabah, and the Tabieen as their fundamental source. In other words, they all agree that their *theological* code is the foundation of their legal concepts.

It is needless to dwell on the total irrelevancy of such an influence. Theology, while perfectly legitimate in its own domain, can claim no legitimate influence over Private Law, no more than Private Law can over theology. Thus every Mohammedan law-concept is honeycombed in form as it were, or rather stinted in its growth by the conflicting influence of theological ideas.

The Romans, on the other hand, never allowed their religious concepts to interfere with the fundamental features of their Private Law. The Sibylline or sacred books of the Romans were in constant use among them; but only for *political* purposes. The Roman Senate frequently, nay continually, charged certain officers *ad libros ire*, to consult

---

[a] *N. E. Baillie*, Moh. Law of Sale, p. 21.

the sacred books, just as Mohammedan nations refer to the Kooran. But it never occurred to the Senate to consult these mysterious theological books on questions of Private Law. And thus the Private Law of the Romans remained unbiassed by an irrelevant influence that has impeded the growth of a science of Mohammedan Law; and likewise the scientific development of the Private Law of the Hindoos and Jews. For it is evident on the face of the matter, that if a system of Private Law is constantly interfered with by elements alien to the nature of Private Law, its development must needs be retarded and driven into unprofitable directions.

I have finally to say a few words about the relation of Roman Private Law to Ethics. Ethical and moral ideas have largely, and often unduly, influenced the unrestrained growth of Private Law. For although Private Law has close relations with Ethics, it contains and comprises leading ideas distinctly different from ethical ideas. Our obligations to a certain individual are quite different when arising from motives of friendship, and when caused by the duties of a legal contract. In fact the domain of Private Law is widely separated from the domain of Ethics. Ethical obligations the Romans named *officia*, and they had special treatises on them in contradistinction to the obligations of Law. But they never confounded the needs and powers of ethical with those of jural relations. And thus they contrived to develop the principles of their Private Law undisturbed and unbiassed by factors of an alien kind.

It is therefore that their legal principles have that comprehensiveness and thoroughgoing character which is the great glory of Roman Law. A Roman lawyer, and even a modern French or German lawyer—French and German Private Law being essentially Roman Law—were, and are, never obliged to ransack whole libraries ot precedents to find the law covering a given case. They approach a case in the manner of a physician: carefully informing themselves of the facts underlying the case, and then eliciting the legal spark by means of close meditation on the given data according to the general principles of their science. The *Corpus juris civilis* is one stout volume. This one volume has sufficed to cover billions of cases during more than thirteen centuries. The principles laid down in this volume will afford ready help in almost every case of Private Law, because they emanate from Private Law alone, and have no tincture of non-legal elements. The law of the English, for instance, is so intimately connected with English feudalism and the constitution of England, that unless a country possessed the same kind of, or a similar constitution, it could not adopt one line of English law. The Private Law of the Romans is connected with none of their peculiarly Roman institutions, and consequently it fits the law of any nation, provided this nation wants a science of Private Law, which is not always the case.

This statement seems to lack all historical evidence. One hour's reading in the Corpus Juris seems to show us any number of peculiarly Roman institutions, that influence largely the structure of Roman Private Law. Such is, for instance, Roman slavery. Now-a-days we have no slaves, and thus one might think that the wonderfully refined speculations of Roman Jurists on questions connected with slave-law—one half of the striking "fragments" of *Africanus* treat of such cases—are all obsolete and can have no bearing on our modern Private Law. I venture to state that the number of cases where slaves are brought into play, forms over 60 per cent. of all cases of the Corpus Juris.

Now according to what we notice in our own law, we should expect, that no modern civilian will devote his time to the intricate questions of Roman slave-law, Roman *patronatus*, Roman *libertini*, &c., &c., just as no English practical jurist will devote his time to a laborious study of old English serf- and villein-law. Roman Law, however, is so independent of institutions peculiarly Roman, that while slavery has long ceased to be of any practical interest to the jurists of modern Europe—except as a pretext to grab large territories in Africa—Roman slave-law continues to exercise a most intense interest, and recent books like Prof. *Leist's* books on " Roman Patronatus " are eagerly welcomed on all hands as contributions to practical law.

In fact, as we shall see in our next lecture, Roman slave-law has a value entirely independent of the historical and as it were accidental institution of Roman slavery. American slavery is a thoroughly historical institution, and the works of *Cobb, Hurd, Wilson* and others on American slave-law are totally ignored by the present lawyers of Louisiana, Alabama or Mississippi. Not so Roman treatises on slave-law.

It is the same case with the peculiarly Roman institution of " Patria potestas," which, although long obsolete as such, is still of practical value to all countries where Roman Law has been adopted, as we shall see in our next lecture.

And thus I trust you will fully grasp the distinctive excellence of Roman Private Law. It grew up in a strictly legal atmosphere, and consequently furnishes us principles of a purely jural and legal character, as distinct from law-principles tinctured with political, theological, or ethical concepts; it developed as Pomponius once says : " *rebus ipsis dictantibus.*"

We have now to inquire what was the originating cause,

the *vera causa* of this marvellous Law? Why was it that the Romans alone were able to furnish their age and all subsequent ages with law-principles that were as completely divested of non-legal elements as are the propositions in Euclid of non-mathematical? Before proceeding to a sketch of my view of the *vera causa*, it will be necessary to premise the views of others.

In his well-known book on Greek and Roman commonwealths, the late Prof. Fustel de Coulanges expresses himself concerning the origin of Roman Law as follows : " Quand nous avons parlé plus haut de l'organisation de la famille et des lois grecques ou romaines qui réglaient la propriété, la succession, le testament, l'adoption, nous avons observé combien ces lois correspondaient exactement aux croyances des anciennes générations. Si l'on met ces lois en présence de l'équité naturelle, on les trouve souvent en contradiction avec elle, et il paraît assez évident que ce n'est pas dans la notion du droit absolu et dans le sentiment du juste qu'on est allé les chercher. Mais que l'on mette ces mêmes lois en regard du culte des morts et du foyer, qu'on les compare aux diverses prescriptions de cette religion primitive, et l'on reconnaîtra qu'elles sont avec tout cela dans un accord parfait." ("La Cité Antique," liv. III., ch. xi.)

In other words, according to Coulanges, Roman as well as Greek Law was derived from the religious beliefs of the Romans and Greeks, from the worship of their ancestors and their homesteads. This explanation of the origin of Roman Law fails to account for the very first question involved in our problem : namely, why the Greeks were unable to create the very elements of a law-system which the Romans succeeded to bring to the highest pitch of perfection. Prof. Coulanges' explanation covers both Greeks and Romans ; it tries to account for the law of the former as well as for that of the latter, taking it for granted

that there is no essential difference between Greek and
Roman Law, as there was no essential difference between
their religious beliefs. But this is exactly the thing that
we are forced to deny. Roman Law is essentially, and as
the Latin saying is, *toto cœlo* different from Greek Law;
consequently it cannot be derived from religious beliefs the
majority of which were common both to Greeks and
Romans. In fact, as I have endeavoured to suggest,
Roman Law owns its excellence partly to the fact of its
being entirely independent of religious ideas.

Prof. Ihering, of Göttingen, in Germany, in his cele-
brated work entitled, "Geist des römischen Rechts,"—
"Spirit of Roman Law" (or, as some of his opponents
have put it, "Spirit of Prof. Ihering"), says a good deal
about the causes of Roman Law; he thinks that the cultivation of law was allotted to the Romans, "according to
the economy of History [b]." This very probably means,
that the Romans had a historical vocation to cultivate law,
because—they were given the power to do so. This again
is on a line with the assertion that the poverty in London,
for instance, is owing to the great number of poor people
in London. And this again means nothing at all. To say
that a nation performed certain feats of intellect or character,
because it had a historical vocation for it, is tantamount
to a confession of total ignorance regarding the causes
of such feats. Ihering proceeds to say that the Roman
people had one pre-eminent trait of character, *selfishness;*
and that their law is—the religion of selfishness [c]. And
this peculiar trait of character made them apt to carry
out the promptings of their historical vocation. "The
Roman world taken as a whole may be designated as
the triumph of the idea of utilitarianism and practicability;

[b] "Nach der Oekonomie der Geschichte" (I., p. 316).
[c] "Die Religion der Selbstsucht" (*ib.*, p. 328).

all her forces both of mind and character exist on behalf of utilitarian objects. Selfishness is the moving power of the whole ; the whole of Roman virtues and institutions is the objectivation or the organism of national selfishness [d]." Having thus characterised the Roman nation he proceeds to gather the infinitude of Roman law-institutions under a few heads which he calls " Principles " or leading ideas, first of which is the "principle" of the "subjective will," and of this he says that it is the fountain-head of Roman Law. In addition to this he teaches that there were several " Triebe " or propensities at work, and he deduces many Roman law-concepts from such national propensities.

I am sorry to say that while I readily accept many of Prof. Ihering's brilliant suggestions, especially in the last volume of his work, I fail to see the adequacy of his vague " principles " and " propensities." I most profoundly believe that such terms are nothing else than the *"qualitates occultae"* of the scholastics, that they do not account for concrete institutions, and that they can at the best only characterise an institution, but not deduce it from its real causes. True, the Roman nation manifests a certain selfishness, although it is hard to see why we should blame a nation for selfishness, every single member of which laboured more for the common weal than for his own profit. But one or two moral traits are totally unfit to account for concrete institutions.

[d] " Die römische Welt, im Ganzen und Grossen erfasst, lässt sich mit einem Wort als der Triumph der Idee der Zweckmässigkeit bezeichnen ; sie selbst so wie alle intellectuellen und moralischen Kräfte die innerhalb derselben thätig werden, sind der Zwecke wegen da, mit Rücksicht auf sie bestimmt und gestaltet. Die Selbstsucht ist die Triebfeder des Ganzen ; jene ganze Schöpfung mit allen ihren Institutionen und allen den Tugenden, die sich an ihr bethätigen, ist nichts als die Objectivirung oder der Organismus der nationalen Selbstsucht." (I., 324.)

The Greeks surely can be said to have been a people with a keen sense of beauty. But who will explain the rise of their marvellous sculpture from this sense alone? Who will call it the fountain-head of their sculpture? In other words, Who will call a symptom a cause? Time forbids me to enter into details, but I may be allowed to say that the Romans were not one whit more selfish than any other nation, and that the principle of subjective will was not stronger in them than in any other prosperous people.

The late Sir H. Maine (in the first chapter of his " Ancient Law ") was of opinion that Roman Law owed its peculiar development to the " theoretical descent of Roman jurisprudence from a code," meaning the XII. Tables, and that "the theoretical ascription of English Law to immemorial unwritten tradition " was the chief reason of its developing differently from Roman Law. He lays particular stress on the fact that the Romans possessed a code at a time when usage was still wholesome, as he says. In fact, he thinks that the XII. Tables were the chief cause of Roman Law having so steadily advanced to its ultimate perfection. I regret to say that I cannot accept this as an adequate explanation. The XII. Tables were an admirable collection of the current law of the fourth and fifth decades of the fifth century B.C. But so were the codes of the Icelanders, Irish, Welsh, or Germans. They all had codes, and at a very early date of their history. But not one of those nations succeeded in developing the original code to a perfect system of Law. Why should a code as such be productive of this result? Can a code not become obsolete, inconvenient, and inapplicable? The marvel is not that the Romans once had a code, called the XII. Tables, but that they. persistently clung to it for over eight centuries, although continually improving and refining upon it. This tenacious and pious attachment to a code can surely not be explained by the code itself. It originates not from the code but from the people who uphold it. The Americans continue to observe their written constitution, not because it was once written, but because *they* are determined to revere it as their fundamental law. It is their merit, not that of Jefferson or Washington.

Prof. Theodor Mommsen, of Berlin, in his "Roman History," devotes several chapters to the consideration of Roman Law, and occasionally he gives the following solution of our problem :—" It is customary to laud the Romans as a nation privileged to the cultivation of law, and to admire their excellent law as a mystical gift from Heaven ; this is probably done to save us feeling ashamed of the misery of our own administration of law. One glance at the extremely inconsistent and undeveloped criminal law of the Romans should convince of the untenableness of their vague notions regarding Roman Law, even those to whom it would appear too simple to say, that a sound nation has a sound law, and an ill nation an unsound e." In other words : the simple solution of the mystery of the law of the Romans, according to Prof. Mommsen, is the fact that they were a healthy nation, and, accordingly, had a healthy law. In the passage just quoted from Mommsen, he animadverts on the highly imperfect state of Roman

* "Man pflegt die Römer als das zur Jurisprudenz privilegirte Volk zu preisen und ihr vortreffliches Recht als eine mystische Gabe des Himmels anzustaunen ; vermuthlich besonders um sich die Scham zu ersparen über die Nichtswürdigkeit des eigenen Rechtzustandes. Ein Blick auf das beispiellos schwankende und unentwickelte römische Criminalrecht könnte von der Unhaltbarkeit dieser unklaren Vorstellungen auch diejenigen überzeugen, denen der Satz zu einfach erscheinen möchte, dass ein gesundes Volk ein gesundes Recht hat und ein krankes ein krankes." ("Recht" in vol. I. Röm. Gesch.)

criminal law; how shall we now understand his "healthiness of the Romans?" They had a good civil law, because they were a healthy nation. Why then did they not also have a good criminal law? His expression "sound law" refers both to civil and criminal law. If a healthy nation have a healthy law, why not a healthy criminal law as well as a healthy civil law? But apart from this insoluble contradiction, what shall such an extremely vague and cloudy statement avail us? Were the Spartans not a healthy nation? And the Macedonians? Health is a very valuable thing both in individuals and nations; but health alone cannot account for concrete achievements in science or philosophy. The health of a nation depends chiefly on a sound condition of its finances and its army, together with the purity of family life and public morals. I fail to see how these factors can account for the fact that the Romans alone produced a perfect system of Private Law. Many another nation had sound financial, military, and moral conditions; but the Romans alone created an immortal system of Private Law.

I shall now try to draw the outlines of my view of the real causes of Roman Private Law. The search for such causes is frequently discredited at the hands of some jurists, as savouring too much of metaphysical, or purely philosophical ideas. And as a rule the authors of histories of Roman Law carefully avoid investigating the causes of the grand fabric of the Law they treat of. The Romans themselves had no idea of the real motors of their law, and this is perfectly in keeping with the experience of our own times. Very few Englishmen could give a satisfactory account of the rise of English Equity Law, barring mere quotations from the current histories of English Law. Or to come to present times, exceedingly few Englishmen or Americans could satisfactorily account for the rise of two recent social movements that have already assumed vast dimensions. I mean Prohibitionism and the Salvation Army. The modern historians of Roman Law, not being able to find *explicit* passages of Roman authors concerning the real causes of their Law, simply ignore the questions, and remain, as Rudorff says, "on the ground of solid comprehension and continuous work [f]."

Rudorff and many more German historians of Roman Law notwithstanding, I venture to say that unless we can fully comprehend the *practical* causes that were productive of Roman Law, we shall never be able to understand the institutions of Roman Law as we understand some of our own institutions. They will never come home to us; they will only be an undigested mass of learned texts, which we have to commit to memory through laborious study of the ancient and modern authorities. A clear understanding of the causes of Roman Law, on the other hand, facilitates our study of that Law most effectively. In order to convey a very distinct idea of my view I have tried to reduce it to a few words, in fact, to one single word, so that whatever you may happen to think of the value of my view, you will not be doubtful as to what my view is.

The main cause of the rise of Roman Private Law and its high perfection I take to be the Roman institution of Infamia.

The Roman institution of *Infamia* was the fountain-head, or rather the chief motor and factor that brought about the majority of those legal institutions the sum total of which go to form the system of Roman Law. It was this institution that led to the rise of Roman jurists; not of lawyers, but of *jurisprudentes;* and it was likewise this institution that served these jurists with a mental check, as it were, in

[f] "Auf dem Boden soliden Erkennens und Fortarbeitens." (*Rechtsgesch.* Preface.)

their elaboration of legal concepts. To bear out this assertion I shall first characterise in a few words the institution of Roman *Infamia.*

Infamia in Latin means infamy, public disgrace. *Savigny*, whose chapter on *Infamia* is still considered the best exstant treatise on this institution, says: "Infamia as the consequence of a criminal sentence became a general rule only by degrees [g]." And this is the salient point of the whole problem, the point to which I wish you to pay special attention. Certain trespasses entailed the punishment of public disgrace. The Romans, just as we, punished certain trespasses or offences with fines and loss of honour. A person convicted of theft is considered disgraced in our times. He is unable to hold a public office, and society will not receive him. That, therefore, the Romans were sensible of the disgrace inherent in certain offences appears very natural indeed.

/ But what shall we say on reading that the Romans did not think that a person was disgraced by embezzling public money? or committing a crime against public morals? For such is the case. We read in *Zumpt's* "Criminal Law of the Roman Republic:" "There is no trace that persons fined by the Tribunes had to suffer from any public disgrace; on the contrary, there are examples of such persons having kept their offices [h]," and he quotes several examples of Roman officials who were convicted of embezzling public money and yet did not sustain any loss of honour, or *capitis diminutio.*

[g] "[Infamie wegen] Verurtheilung eines Kriminalverbrechens wurde erst nach und nach zu einer allgemeinen Regel ausgebildet." (*Systhem* II., § 77.)

[h] "Es findet sich nirgends die geringste Spur, dass die durch die Tribunen zu Geldstrafen Verurtheilten irgend eine öffentliche Schande erlitten, dagegen Beispiele wo dieselben in ihrer Stellung verblieben." (I., 2, pp. 293—312.)

This strange leniency stands in glaring contrast with the utter rigour of Roman Law concerning trespasses or offences of a much lesser kind. In fact it is no paradox at all to say that while the Romans of the Republic readily connived at some of the most dangerous offences committed against the commonwealth of Rome, they mercilessly resented the slightest rupture of *private* relations. In other words : *their private law was infinitely more draconic than their criminal law.* We just saw that an embezzler of public money was fined but not disgraced. On the other hand, we learn that a private agent of a Roman, a *mandatarius*, if there was a *civil* judgment against him enjoining him to refund the money he had been intrusted with, was *ipso facto* disgraced, that is, henceforth unable to vote or to be elected.

Mind the enormity of the case : there is a civil judgment in a civil case ; a judgment commanding the defendant to refund the money he had received from his mandator. This judgment put an indelible stain on the social life of the defendant; in fact, it made him a social outcast. And now compare the horrible consequence of this *civil* judgment with the indifferent consequence of the criminal conviction of an embezzler of public money ! What inconsistency ! the private agent of a private person is defeated in a civil law-suit ; and instead of being held to pay a fine he is deprived of his most precious civil rights, of rights that were infinitely more precious to a Roman than to a modern "citizen." A Roman who was deprived of his right of suffrage and consequently of his eligibility to the various offices of the state, was deprived of his very life. Outside state-life there was no life in Republican Rome. Death was decidedly preferable to the punishment of *infamia*, and the latter has rightly been called "civil death." And this civil death was the lot of him who had the misfortune of getting

defeated in civil law suits. For the case of an agent was
not the only case in which *infamia* could be inflicted. In
fact, if we endeavour to represent to ourselves the actual
practice of Roman Private Law, we shall see that the
*spectre of Infamia threatened the citizens at nearly every step
of their daily actions.*

Infamia was directly or indirectly the consequence of
innumerable actions. In current works on Roman Law
you will find enumerated a small number of actions that
could bring *infamia* upon the defeated defendant. This,
however, is an altogether misleading statement. *Infamia*
was, for instance, the consequence of *commodatum*, that
is, when a lender sued the borrower, provided the borrower
had used the loaned thing in a way contrary to stipulation.
In such a case the lender could use the *actio furti* which
inflicted *infamia* on the defendant. One of the most
generally applicable actions was the *actio doli*, since it lay
in every case when an evil design on the part of the
defendant could be proved, provided there was no other
specific *actio* applicable. But any civil action could inflict
infamia, inasmuch as the execution of any civil judgment,
or as we call it, any writ of *Fieri facias*, inflicted *infamia*.

It is this fact that gives to some of Cicero's orations in
civil causes—by the way, the best means of getting a
practical insight into the working of Roman Law—their
tragical colouring. Take the oration "*pro Publio Quintio*."
The whole oration hinges on the question whether a writ
of *Fieri facias* had been rightly issued or not. This seems
to us an altogether prosaic affair, and we fail to see why
Cicero makes such a pathetic fuss over it. Just listen to
the following passage, which seems to be part of one of
Seneca's tragedies, and in reality refers to an argument in
a case of money matters: "Quid enim nunc agit Sex.
Naevius [the plaintiff]? Qua de re controversia est? Quod

est hoc judicium, in quo jam biennio versamur? Quid
negotii geritur, in quo ille tot et tales viros defatigat?
Pecuniam petit. Nunc denique? Verumtamen petit.
Audiamus. De rationibus et controversiis societatis vult
dijudicari. Sero. Verum aliquando tamen : concedamus.
Non, inquit, id ago, C. Aquilli [the prætor before whom
Cicero pleaded], neque in eo nunc laboro. Pecunia mea tot
annos utitur P. Quintius; utatur sane : non peto. Quid
igitur pugnas? An, quod saepe multis in locis dixisti, *ne
in civitate sit ? ne locum suum, quem adhuc honestissime
defendit, obtineat ? ne numeretur inter vivos ? decernat de vita
et ornamentis suis omnibus ?"* &c., &c. (cap. 13). Such
language is used in our times when a matter of life and
death is at issue. But was it not a question of life and death
when the whole civil existence of a Roman was at stake?
And so it was [i]. For if Cicero failed to prove that the
prætor's writ of *Fieri facias* had been issued contrary to
the law, his client forthwith lost his political honours, or as
Cicero expresses it, ceased to be amongst the living.

My time precludes any elaborate discussion of the countless possibilities of *infamia* in Republican Rome. May it
suffice to state that *infamia* was the sword of Damocles,
that constantly hung over the life of every single Roman
during the whole period of the Republic. The causes
of this strange institution are patent to any one who carefully studies the marvellous frame of the Roman state.
It is impossible to dwell on this point at present. I will
state this much, that the institution of *infamia* was the great
constitutional check of the Roman Commonwealth. *Infamia* thus threatened every single Roman at every step
and at every turn of his every-day life. He could not
transact the least bit of business, the smallest affair that

In the *Corpus juris* the risk of *infamia* is also compared to the risk
of life; see l. 9, pr. D (*de manumissis vindicta*) XL., 2.

could eventually lead to litigation in court, without jeopardizing his very civil existence.

Now represent to yourself the practical working of such an institution as *infamia*. On the one hand, every Roman citizen was profoundly convinced of the impossibility of shaking off the tyranny of that institution; on the other hand, every Roman citizen could not help seeing that some means have to be discovered which will obviate the sorest consequences of *infamia* without doing away with the otherwise wholesome institution itself. Suppose a Roman had a friend whom he had commissioned to do some business for him; in short, suppose the *mandatarius* of a Roman happened to be his friend. For some reason or other this *mandatarius* could not refund the money he had been intrusted with, or did not wind up his *mandatum* in a proper way. The Roman now is under the obligation to sue his friend with the *actio mandati directa*, that is, with an action that will eventually bring *infamia* upon his friend, or on himself. For, if the judges held that his friend was not bound to refund any money, his friend could sue him with the *actio injuriarum*, which brought likewise *infamia* upon the defeated defendant. As in this case so it was in innumerable cases of every-day life.

Now, no gentleman will delight in ruining his friend for a sum of money. In this predicament of his the Roman naturally turned to some clever man of his acquaintance for advice. This clever man could solve the problem in one way only: not being allowed to uproot the foundations of the institution of *infamia*, that is of *substantive law*, he essayed to compass his end by fitly adapting the case of his client to *adjective* law, to the *law of procedure*. Thus it came about, that that portion of the law of Rome, which we are used to call the adjective or subordinate portion of law, was in reality the substantive portion of it. *In*

Roman Law the law of procedure was the prior, the substantive law. This is exactly the reverse of English law, in which the law of procedure is called adjective law. The *actio* is the moderator of rights, and not *vice versa.*

The common law of Rome was a law in which the action was not the mere appendix of the right, as in modern times, but its root. Now-a-days we distinguish between contentious jurisdiction and voluntary jurisdiction, as it is called in English ecclesiastical law. Conveyancing, e.g., is a non-contentious affair, and consequently it does not assume the garb of an action. But in Rome the most peaceful act of non-contentious transactions assumed the garb of a full-fledged action at law. For in Rome the *actio*, that is contentious law, was the fountain-head of non-contentious law. This is the distinctive character of Roman Law. How this fundamental character, or rather force of Roman Law was conducive to the rise of the several parts of Roman Law, I shall try to discuss in our next lecture. At present it will suffice to have pointed out the *vera causa*, or actual working cause of Roman Law.

For, one moment's reflection will satisfy any student of Roman institutions, that in a commonwealth where ordinary business-transactions were saturated with germs of the most deleterious nature, some citizens will naturally fall to thinking about remedies that might mitigate the virulence of the poison. And this is the reason why the Romans, a military people, a people that held commerce in contempt, and who did not cultivate philosophy or science at all, a people of haughty warriors, who never succeeded in systemizing their constitutional or criminal law—I say, this is the reason why the Romans felt induced to pay such extraordinary attention to the regulation and systematization of Private Law. *Their Private Law had the character not of our Private Law, but of our modern criminal law;* and it is only in the domain of criminal law that we can ever hope to equal the ancient Romans, since our criminal law arises from an institution similar, if not identical, with the institution of *infamia*, namely, the institution of modern social honour.

We can entertain no hopes to equal the Romans in the elaboration of systems of Private Law; but we are allowed to cherish the hope that we shall uphold the fabric of our civilization without placing the sword of Damocles over the head of every citizen in every hour of his daily life. For all higher institutions high prices must be paid. The unrivalled abundance of Greek literature, philosophy, and science was purchased at the expense of the total subjugation of the female and two thirds of the male population of Greece. Roman Law was purchased at the expense of an institution than which the Spanish Inquisition was not much more cruel. Let us charitably hope that our civilization, if wanting in a perfect system of Private Law, is also wanting in social spectres like the Roman institution of *infamia*.

II.

THE *VERA CAUSA* OF ROMAN LAW (*continued*).

Details about the vera causa :—Explanation of the *actiones in factum ;* of praetorian legislation ; of the curious bondage of Roman house-sons (*filiifamilias*) and of *patria potestas ;* of the influence of Roman slavery on the formation of Roman law-concepts.

IN a report of the *Oxford Magazine* of 12th March, 1890, on the preceding lecture it was urged, that the Roman institution of *infamia* could not have played a paramount *rôle* in the formation of Roman jurisprudence, considering that the Athenians had an identical institution—ἀτιμία—but no science of Private Law.

But for *one* circumstance this objection would effectively destroy the force of Roman *infamia* as a *vera causa* of the science of Roman Private Law. This circumstance, however, is fatal : Athenian ἀτιμία was *not* identical with Roman *infamia*. On the contrary, it was in numerous and essential points diametrically opposed to it. Athenian ἀτιμία—the only Greek ἀτιμία of which we possess authoritative knowledge—was a consequence of crimes and trespasses against the State* : Roman *infamia* was, in the earlier part of the

* In the latest dictionary of Greek and Roman Antiquities edited by Daremberg and Saglio, under 'Atimia,' Lelyveldt's monograph on Attic *infamia* is quoted to the effect, that ἀτιμία was inflicted upon the unfaithful bailee of a *private* deposit. A glance at the passage in Lelyveldt, p. 186, suffices to invalidate this statement. Moreover, it

Republic and even later, chiefly a consequence of civil torts against private people. Athenian ἀτιμία was hereditary: Roman *infamia* was not. Athenian ἀτιμία could be temporary and partial: Roman *infamia* could not. Athenian ἀτιμία entailed the confiscation of property: Roman *infamia* did not.

In fact, Athenian ἀτιμία was an essentially different institution. The loss of political rights as a consequence of certain crimes or misdemeanors is an institution with which we meet in innumerable nations. The Romans alone had the peculiarity of entailing such a loss, not only as a consequence of crimes or misdemeanors against the state, but also *and mainly* as a consequence of breach of *civil* contracts. Unless we firmly seize this, the salient feature of the whole question, we shall never thoroughly understand the bearing of *infamia* on Roman jurisprudence. Roman "*civil*" law was permeated and saturated with elements of *criminal* law. This is the central fact in the history of Roman Private Law. By "civil" law we here understand *jus civile* in the technical sense of the term.

The cause of this curious fact does not concern us here. It will suffice to say that the Romans, more than any other nation of antiquity, were in need of a very high standard of civil morality, as it were. Just as the ancient Hebrews were compelled to make up for the total lack of political organization—their theocracy being an extreme form of democracy—by the establishment of a most rigorous standard of *ritualistic* morality in every-day life: even so, and for similar reasons, the Romans were compelled to establish an extremely rigorous standard of *civil* morality

has been amply refuted by Meier-Schömann-Lipsius "Der Attische Process," p. 702. The only action of Attic law, the possible effects of which resemble somewhat Roman *infamia*, was the δίκη ἐξούλης. See *Meier-Schömann-Lipsius*, ib. pp. 665—668, and 965—970.

in every-day life. The least transaction in the business
life of a Roman could eventually lead to the gravest
consequences ; just as a very slight oversight of some of the
countless ritualistic rules could increase the mortal sins of
a Hebrew.

Neither the Romans nor the Hebrews could dispense
with the excessively rigorous demands on their civil or
ritualistic scrupulousness. But, at the same time, they
could not help feeling that such demands cannot be strictly
sustained in the face of changing circumstances, the most
important of which was the rapidly increasing number of
their citizens. Accordingly, they naturally fell to thinking
of a remedy, that would mitigate the more obnoxious evils
of an overstrung standard of morality without materially
reducing the beneficial force thereof.

In other words : they tried to dodge the strict injunc-
tions of their laws.

It is not meant to say, that the whole activity of Roman
jurists and Hebrew rabbis can be summed up in calling it
a successful attempt at dodging the rigour of their laws.
But it may be said in strict accordance with historical facts
that the better part of their activity consisted in at once
upholding the fundamental rigidity and obviating its ex-
crescences. Hence, by the way, the striking similarity of,
the outward appearance and system of the Thalmud and
the Corpus juris, both being in the main collections of the
teachings of jurists, clothed in the form of commentaries
on the *leges* and *edicta*, on the one hand, and the *Old
Testament* and the *Mishnah* on the other.

In the preceding lecture it was tried to prove that
Roman Law was not unduly influenced by Politics, Religion,
or Ethics. Thus having gained an exceedingly favourable
condition towards elaborating a purely legal or—as I
ventured to say—*civilistic* science of Private Law, it was

moreover immensely benefited by the activity of Roman jurists as just described. Or to put it more correctly: the private law of the Romans owed its freedom from irrelevant and undue influences on the part of Religion, Politics and Ethics to general and impersonal causes, which it is not incumbent on me to trace on this occasion ; but its freedom from the overpowering influence of criminal law-concepts it owed mainly to the activity of the Roman jurists.

On the continent of Europe the distinction between civil and criminal law is considered a matter of such elementary character, that it rarely occurs to continental jurists, that this distinction is the exception, not the rule, with the majority of nations. The greater portion of civilized and uncivilized nations does not draw a sufficiently sharp line of demarcation between civil and criminal law. Thus in English and American law the trespasses called "torts" partake both of civil and criminal character, and many a merely civil act or omission entails criminal consequences, as in the law of "contempt of court," an institution strikingly similar to, although less comprehensive than, Roman *infamia.*

To continental jurists, therefore, the marked separation of civil from criminal matters in Roman Law seems so natural as to render all further investigation of its causes superfluous. The neglect of this investigation, however, is the cause of very serious shortcomings in the works of continental historians of Roman Law. Instead of dwelling on the fact that the Roman jurists, in divesting the Private Law of Rome of the last of the undue influences to which law has been subject with other nations, contributed powerfully to its final and strictly systematic formation : the continental historians either indulge in mere accumulations of data, or in historico-philosophical constructions of the wildest cast. I venture to say that no writer on natural science, this side of Buffon, has had the courage to publish a book so utterly fantastical as is, for instance, Professor Huschke's book on the constitution of *Servius Tullius.*

It seems strange that the colossal influence of *infamia*, as here described, should not have been noticed by former scholars. This difficulty, however, is easily met by the fact, that previous to *Burchardi's* treatise on *infamia* (1819), and especially, *Savigny's* chapters in his "*Systhem*," the generally prevailing notion of *infamia* was totally unfit to convey a just sense of the immense bearing of that institution on the formation of Roman jurisprudence. And even now few civilians stop to think of the indirect and incessant influence of that institution. In order, therefore, to give a clear, if very succinct, statement of the decisive influence of *infamia* on the formation of Roman jurisprudence, I shall essay to trace this influence in some of the leading groups of Roman law-concepts.

A word or two about *infamia* before descending into the details of our question.

Infamia was the loss of civil rights, of the *jus honorum et suffragii.* In other words: the person tainted with *infamia* was blotted out of the *public* and *political* life of Rome. He could stay in Rome; he could continue to ply his trade and sue his debtors in Rome; will his property, or marry a Roman woman. But in his *public* existence he was not only curtailed, but actually destroyed. He had no vote; he was not eligible to an office.

This was the essence of *infamia.* Here is not the place to explain why the Romans of the Republic, and even to a great extent those of the Empire, dreaded nothing so much as the loss of their rights of suffrage and eligibility. We have to take it as a fact conceded on all hands, at least for the times of the Republic.

If, therefore, the stain of *infamia* was dreaded above everything; and if, on the other hand, the danger of being afflicted with *infamia* was a consequence not of rare or base crimes limited to a small number of evil doers, but entailed on actions of common and daily occurrence: it was a mere matter of pressing necessity that the Romans developed every single institution of their law in a *twofold* form, in a dichotomous arrangement, namely, one according to the strict exigencies of the criminal elements of the *jus civile*, among which *infamia* stands foremost, and another according to the less peremptory and more lenient demands of practical life.

This thoroughgoing dichotomy of Roman Law is one of its chief characteristics. One half of Roman Private Law belongs to the division "*Jus;*" the other half belongs to the division "*Factum.*"

In English common law as well as in continental *criminal* law, the terms "law" and "fact" are very familiar, and no mistake is more difficult to avoid than that of substituting the modern concepts of "law" and "fact" to their Roman synonyms. But the modern "consul" is not more different from the Roman consul than are "law and fact" from Roman "*jus*" and "*factum.*"

The Roman "*Jus*" as contrasted with "*Factum*" has a technical sense of its own. It denotes those institutions of Roman Law that applied strictly and exclusively to the free and independent Roman citizen, or, as the Roman jurists called him, to the *homo sui juris*. Along with the *homo sui juris* there was a great variety of other persons in a state of more or less absolute dependence: the house-sons (*filiifamilias*), the married women, the daughters, the freedmen, the *Latini Juniani*, the *dediticii*, and finally the slaves, and provincials, or *peregrini*. The institutions of Roman Law applicable not only to the *homo sui juris*, but also

to the dependent persons just enumerated, constituted the
" *Factum* " or second division of Roman Law.

" *Factum* " in this the technical sense of the term cannot
be found *explicitly* in the writings of Roman jurists. This,
however, is no objection whatever to its being an appro-
priate term. Thus nothing is more familiar to modern
civilians than the term *actiones stricti juris* as distinguished from *actiones bonae fidei,* yet we all know that the
term *actio stricti juris* does not occur in the writings of
Roman jurists [b].

Nor does the general division of Roman Law into
" *Jus* " and " *Factum* " bear any resemblance to the English division of Law into " *Common Law* " and " *Equity
Law.*" " *Jus* " and " *Factum* " stand in close and intimate relation to *jus civile* and *jus honorarium,* and although the latter emanated from the praetor,—or rather
from the jurists who formed the praetor's *consilium,*—and
although the praetor in Rome displays a striking affinity
with the English Chancellor, the fountain-head of English
Equity Law, yet Roman " *Factum* " is neither co-extensive
with nor essentially related to English " Equity." The
very gist of the contrast between " *Jus* " and " *Factum* "
lies in the thoroughgoing distinction between such persons
as are entitled to the institutions of " Jus " and such as
are not. This distinction is entirely meaningless when
applied to the divergence between " Common Law " and
" Equity."

The free and independent Roman citizen enjoyed such
immense privileges, his citizenship possessed—as we shall
see in a subsequent lecture—such an extraordinary value,
that it was only both fair and natural that his personal
conduct in private and public life should be subjected
to a most rigorous superintendence. Accordingly the law

[b] *Savigny, Systhem,* vol. v. p. 461.

referring to him was saturated with elements of constant
danger to, and imminent risks of the great privileges of
his position. This law was called "*jus*," or "*jus civile.*"
This law is stern, rigid, and almost as implacable as the
doctrines of Calvinism, which were likewise based on
a conception of life, if a future life, according to which
the Christian man may risk eternal damnation by neglect-
ing duties which in less rigorous creeds are held unimportant.

But it will be objected that the Roman house-son was
not debarred from the enjoyment of the great *political*
privileges of the *homo sui juris*, and yet the *jus civile* or
"*jus*" proper was not applicable to him in its entirety.
For, a Roman *filiusfamilias*, while still under the tutelage
of his father, could fill any of the high posts of honour
and power in Rome : he could become quaestor, praetor,
consul, censor, he could vote in the assembly, he could
be sent to the provinces as governor, &c.

Whence this deviation from the principle underlying
the fundamental distinction between *jus* and *factum*? If
this distinction was owing to the privileged position of
. the *homo sui juris*, why did it not hold good also with
regard to house-sons (*filiifamilias*) who enjoyed all the
political privileges of a free and independent Roman
citizen ?

We say political privileges, because it is a well-known
fact, that in his private life, and more especially in his
economical transactions, a Roman house-son was utterly
dependent on his father, down to the end of the Republic,
and, to a very great extent, even during the Empire. A
Roman house-son could not acquire one penny's worth of
property for himself; every thing he acquired belonged
to his father. In that startling dependence nothing was
changed by his political position ; he could be a consul,

a senator or praetor, yet unless his father had formally emancipated him he could not call one farthing his own. In other words : the Roman *patria potestas*, in its civil aspects, means a total disfranchisement of house-sons, who could nevertheless fill the highest posts of honour in the commonwealth.

If, now, we discard all childish considerations, such as "*patriarchal period*," "*race-character*," or similar vagaries ; and if we firmly hold to the self-evident belief in the substantial identity of human nature in all periods of history, we shall naturally ask : Why did Roman house-sons submit to a tyranny than which nothing seems more insupportable to our feeling ? For, surely, the most pressing desire of every well-balanced young man of our time goes toward financial independence, and much as we all love our fathers, we crave for nothing more intensely than for earning our own living, and owning the proceeds of our industry and skill. Consequently we are bound to assume that the young men of Rome must have been prompted by the same wishes, and if, to our astonishment, we find them quite indifferent to a condition of things that seems almost revolting to us, we have to find out the reasons and causes of such an apparent deviation from the ordinary course of human nature. In this inquiry we must never lose sight of that general and irrefragable principle, that the power of a human desire is effectively counterbalanced or overcome only by an equally strong or stronger power of another desire. Hence we may begin our inquiry into the causes of the *civil* aspects of Roman *patria potestas* with the general question, *What was the powerful motive that induced Roman house-sons to submit ungrudgingly to the tyranny of* patria potestas ?

This question is all the more legitimate because Roman house-sons could have easily managed to get rid of the

tyranny of *patria potestas.* Sons, as a general rule, are
always more numerous than fathers; or, at least, the
number of sons in one and the same commonwealth will
frequently exceed the number of fathers. Hence Roman
house-sons, disposing, as they did, of a majority of votes in
the assembly, could have easily passed a law to the effect
that *patria potestas* ceases with the twenty-first or any other
year of the son. Why did they never so much as attempt
to carry such a law? What motive rendered them so
exceedingly submissive?

The excessive value they set upon their citizenship.

The Roman commonwealth was a democracy, in which,
as in all democracies, the fundamental principle of universal suffrage was eluded by a system of organized voting
in classes. The voters of the first class recruited themselves from citizens possessing a certain wealth; the voters
of the second class were citizens possessing a lesser wealth;
and so forth. In addition to this class-arrangement, the
first and second classes voted first, and since they had, as
a rule, the majority of votes,—a vote being the collective
result of the polling of a *centuria*, or subdivision of a class,—
the lower or poorer classes seldom had a chance to cast
a vote.

In other words, Rome was a timocracy. Even after the
class organization of the voters was somewhat changed
through the combination of the *comitia centuriata* with
the *comitia tributa,* the timocratic element of the Roman
commonwealth continued to be predominant. Honour
and power thus being dependent on the census, it was
the ruling desire of every Roman to belong to the higher
or wealthier "classes." To have a high census was equivalent to belonging to the really influential classes. If
now a Roman father had three sons, and each of these
four persons should have shifted for himself, not one of

them would have, in the majority of cases, been fortunate enough to come up to the necessary census. But if the sons, both in their own and in their fathers' interest, desisted from owning what they acquired, the property of the father could much more easily reach and retain the level required by the census of the higher classes, and since sons voted in the class of their father, they participated in a power which they most fervently coveted, but which their isolated efforts could not have secured for them.

Thus the strong motive of economical independence was overpowered by the still stronger motive of ambition. A Roman possessed only one kind of ambition : political. To be an influential member of the *comitia*, to fill one of the offices of the state, to be senator or general of the army were the chief objects of his ambition. To be baulked of the competition for these prizes was practically tantamount to being *infamis*, the very essence of *infamia* being the exclusion from the political arena.

The strange institution of the Roman *patria potestas*, in its civil aspects, therefore, was a direct consequence of the dread of *infamia*, or what was equivalent thereto. The breach in the general principle of dichotomy,— "*Jus*" and "*Factum*,"—was thus due to the very working of this principle, and hence the contradiction between the political independence of the Roman house-son and his economical dependence on his father,—or in other words, the contradiction between his just claim to the division of "*Jus*" and his classification under "*Factum*," is only apparent. House-sons could not acquire for themselves, they could not own; but they could contract debts—and, with few allowances for money-debts—be sued for debts, and in innumerable cases sue their debtors, as we shall see later on.

Infamia also explains another strange principle of Roman Private Law. The jurists of Rome teach us that nobody can acquire rights through the instrumentality of a *free* person : *Per liberam personam adquiri non potest.* Roman Law discourages the use of agents and representatives. The law of a few other nations has similar prohibitions; thus in ancient Egypt *procuratores* were not allowed for sales [c]. The reasons of the Egyptian Law are not known to us; but those of the law of Rome are patent. In a commonwealth where the smallest transaction of every-day life was to carry with it possibilities of a grave responsibility, the law was naturally loth to lightening the burden of such responsibility by a permission to shift the transaction from the shoulders of the persons really engaged in it to a mere go-between, who would risk no responsibility of his own, and stave off the danger of his employer. I said that Roman Private *Jus* is permeated with elements of criminal law. Just as in criminal law representation is utterly inadmissible, every man having to maintain his own cause, even so in Roman Private *Jus* an easy representability is totally incompatible with the very nature of the law. In fact, what could have been easier than to elude the whole fundamental institution of *infamia* by settling one's business affairs through brokers and agents? The agent, *procurator*, could not have suffered *infamia*, since it was not *his* business; the bailor or employer would have been equally exempt from it, since the judgment entailing *infamia* was not given in his name [d]. This is the real explanation of this principle of Roman Law, and explanations like that of M. Schlossman, who accounts for the prohibition of agents in Roman Law by an alleged and " hitherto undiscovered principle pervading the whole body of that law,

[c] See *E. Revillout, Les Obligations en droit Egyptien*, p. 2.
[d] Compare *Savigny, Systhem,* vol. ii. p. 175.

namely, that the economical existence of a free man shall not be absorbed by the economical dealings of another man ͤ," miss the point completely.

A thorough appreciation of the actual working of Roman *infamia* and its correlate institutions alone will enable us to understand properly the immense value of Roman *slaves* as subjects of jurisprudence. In our preceding lecture I broached the question, why American slavery has long since ceased to be an object of interest to American jurists, whereas Roman slavery, or the vast number of slave-cases in the *Corpus juris civilis,* has to the present day lost nothing of its significance, although the institution of slavery itself is of no practical moment.

Roman Law has two great types, complementary and supplementary to one another : the *homo sui juris* and the *servus,* or slave. How great soever our ethical or religious horror of slavery may be, how very little soever we should feel inclined to credit a hateful institution with products the glory of which we cannot deny : the sober, historical truth of these two types cannot be denied. The Roman slave is not merely the beast of burden, the despised " nigger " of America, the alleged "machine " of Roman antiquity. He occupied an exceedingly important space in the meditations of Roman jurists. Even the lawyers and jurists of the Slave-states of the Union previous to the civil war could not help noticing a certain number of odd and intensely interesting legal problems arising from the *status* of slavery, that is to say, from the combination of "object" (*res*) and subject in one and the same being. Thus they wonder how to decide the odd problem as to what has to happen when one of two joint owners of a slave emancipates the latter? Or what shall be the law regarding fugitive slaves? And similar puzzles. But they never

ͤ *Schlossmann, Der Besitzerwerb durch Dritte,* Pref., p. vi.

attempted or deemed it necessary to attempt a comprehensive jural construction of all the civil relations of slaves.
The Roman jurists, on the other hand, traced out with
marvellous ingenuity and unparalleled perseverance, the
subtlest ramifications of civil slave-law. All the puzzling
and profoundly interesting relations of slaves in their
various capacities as agents, debtors, creditors, fathers,
sons, kinsmen, heirs, legatees, public officers, private in-
structors, and even as corpses,—a slave's burial-place being
declared sacred,—the Roman jurists elaborated with the
carefulness of devotees. Look at the slave-law of the
Hebrews, as told by *M. Mielziener* or *J. Winter*, or at the
slave-law of the Germans or Anglo-Saxons : how meagre
and stale it appears beside the full-grown plasticity of
Roman slave-law.

Whence this profound interest in people whom as a class
they apparently despised?

It was an interest dictated by a most pressing want :
the want of those remedies that were to counteract or
check the gravest consequences of *infamia*, and correlate
institutions. In a commonwealth where *jus plenum* was
the privilege of comparatively few independent citizens ;
where, as a consequence, the jural construction of civil
transactions was largely dependent on the solution of
preliminary questions, to wit, whether the persons engaged
in the transaction had or had not a right to transact the
business, and how far their right was qualified by their
condition : in such a commonwealth the theoretical as well
as practical importance of slaves is a matter of course.
A Roman citizen was impeded by a great number of trammels in his civil transactions. Even the *homo sui juris* was
not capable of or lost some rights by being a minor, or a
capite minutus, or an *infamis*. Dependent persons, as house-
sons, women, freedmen, adopted persons, or independent

strangers,—*peregrini,*—and corporations, in addition to the restrictions of *pubertas,* minor age, and *infamia* were unable to do a great number of transactions in their own name. The constant recurrence of these impediments rendered the jural construction of a given case an arduous task. On the other hand, the most superficial observer of Roman life could not avoid noticing the immense advantage offered by the peculiar character of the slaves of Rome. Roman slaves were, with few exceptions, white, intelligent people, entrusted with all descriptions of business and professions, both material, financial, and intellectual. In other words: they moved and acted exactly like free Roman citizens in all the walks of life, politics excepted. They carried on the bulk of the civil business transactions of their masters ; they carried on a very considerable amount of their own business, by means of *peculia* granted them by their masters ; they were prospective free men.

But as long as they remained slaves they were free from the very trammels that stood in the way of a complete jural construction of civil transactions. A Roman slave *in point of law* was neither a minor, nor did he ever come of age ; neither an *infamis,* nor a *capite minutus ;* neither a *filius-familias,* nor a *peregrinus ;* neither a father or husband, nor a son : he was a *res,* an object. Yet he behaved and acted as if he were a free person. The Roman jurist, therefore, when in need of studying a jural relation untrammelled by the restrictions so numerous with free persons, naturally turned to a case where a slave was the acting person, such a case being entirely free from all extraneous influences. For, the legal incapacity of a Roman slave was not a derivative incapacity, a mere consequence of his master's *potestas ;* it was an original incapacity, extending, as it did, even to abandoned slaves without masters. Roman slaves were, from the standpoint of the jurist, the peers and strictly correlate and complementary types of the *homo sui juris*. They alone could satisfy the want of Roman jurists for unalloyed cases of purely civil relations.

And was there a more pressing want in Rome? The theoretical and practical basis of their commonwealth was a civil law saturated with the spirit of criminal law; the lasting feasibleness of such a commonwealth depended on a refined secretion of these criminal elements, or, in other words, in the elaboration of a science of purely civil private law. To this end nothing was more conducive than the jural relations of slaves. Shall we then wonder at the intense interest of Roman jurists in slave-law?

The Germanic nations, as also the French and Slav peoples, had a great number of trammels of personality, such as we meet with in Roman Law. They also had slaves. But they had no need whatever for a science of purely civil private law, their private law standing quite apart from their criminal law, and not being closely allied to their political constitution.

Or to put it still briefer: The Roman jurists, who found the *homo sui juris* an untractable subject for the study of purely civil jural relations, were in constant need of a *homo—pur et simple.* This they found in the Roman slave; *homo* is the usual designation of a slave in their writings.

This also explains the undying interest of modern jurists in the Roman slave. This interest is but the counterpart of our interest in the *homo sui juris*, in the Roman independent citizen. Roman slaves do not occupy a small and out-of-the-way nook in the splendid edifice of Roman Private Law; they form part and parcel of the mighty granite-blocks on which that edifice is reared. Their business relations to their own masters were treated like business relations between free Romans, and the Roman Law concerning the *causa* of contracts applied to slaves as well as to free citizens [f]. As a creditor or debtor his *obligatio* was only *naturalis*, that is,· not endowed with the force of a *civilis obligatio*. But *Donellus* rightly remarks, that *"generaliter recte definiemus, quicumque civilis obligationis justae et ad exigendum efficacis effectus sunt, eosdem esse et naturalis obligationis, una actione demta* [g]." This shows clearly the thoroughgoing parallelism between transactions of slaves and free men. The fundamental dichotomy of Roman Law mentioned above knew of no more momentous question than that regarding the *"jus"* or *"factum"* character of a jural relation. Is *possessio* a *jus* or a *factum?* And *ususfructus* or *usus?* In a vast number of such questions Roman slavery furnished the requisite answer. Thus the fact, that even slaves cannot acquire *possessio* for their masters *"nisi volentibus,"* whereas the acquisition of *dominium* for their masters did not depend on that restriction, clearly shows the *factum*-character of *possessio*, since *factum non egreditur personam* [h]. Likewise *ususfructus* could form the *legatum* to a slave ; *usus* could not, for evident reasons. Hence *ususfructus* was rather a *res facti*,—since *facti, non juris capaces sunt servi*—and *usus* a *res juris*. Consequently *usus* was indivisible, *ususfructus* divisible, &c.

We can now bring our appreciation of Roman slavery as a subject-matter of private law to its final issue. The thoroughgoing principle of dichotomy in Roman Law, the relation of *"Jus"* and *"Factum,"* was shown in its unison in the *homo sui juris*, and in its antithesis in the slave. The former represented *Factum* and *Jus*, the latter *Factum*

---

[f] "Ut debitor vel servus domino, vel dominus servo intelligatur, ex *causa civili* computandum est," l. 49, § 2, D (de peculio) XV., i. Compare *Savigny, Systh.* II., p. 422 and 423.

[g] *Hugo Donellus, Commentarii de jure civili,* lib. XII., cap. 2.

[h] See *H. Donellus, Commentarii,* lib. v., cap. 8 and 9 ; and especially the l. 44, pr. D (de acqu. et amiss. possessione) XLI., 2.

without *Jus.* Hence the lasting importance of the Roman slave; he forms not merely an *historical* category in the development of Roman Private Law, but a *dogmatical* element thereof[1].

The working of *infamia* and correlate institutions like-wise accounts for that strange division of objects in Roman Law in *res mancipi,* and *res nec mancipi.* This division repeats the type of *jus* and *factum* in objects, just as the division in *homo sui juris* and *homo alieni juris* represents the same type in persons.

But it is in the actions of Roman Law where the vast influence of *infamia* and correlate institutions shows best. We now know that the most general division of actions in Roman Law was in *actiones in jus conceptae,* and *actiones in factum conceptae.* Ever since the discovery of the commentaries of Gaius by Niebuhr in the beginning of this century, the historians of Roman Law have endeavoured to explain this dichotomy of actions. Time forbids me to enter into an examination of their theories; I can only advance my own view on this moot question. The actual cause of these two classes of actions I take to be the desire of Roman jurists to obviate the grave and avoidable conse-quences of *infamia* and correlate institutions, in the civil law-suits of Roman citizens.

---

[1] We here subjoin a number of dogmatically typical slave-cases from the writings of *Labeo* alone; they are all taken from the Pandects: l. 34, I., 7;—l. 4, § 3, II., 4;—l. 1, § 1, II., 9;—l. 9, § 1, II., 11;—l 4, § 2, II., 13;—l. 27, pr., III., 3;—l. 6, § 6, III., 5;—l. 18, § 2, eod;—l. 7, § 7, IV., 3;—l. 2, § 1, eod;—l. 20, pr., eod;—l. 13, pr., IV., 6;—l. 19, § 3, V., 1;—l. 21, VII., 1;—l. 2, § 1, VII., 8;—l. 10, § 4, eod;—l. 12, § 6, eod;—l. 13, eod;—l. 23, § 4, IX., 2;—l. 24, IX., 4;—l. 26, § 5, eod;—l. 15, XII., 4;—l. 5, § 7, XIV., 3;—l. 5, § 8, eod;—l. 5, § 9, eod;—l. 5, § 7, XIV., 4;—l. 5, § 13, eod.;—l. 7, § 4, eod;—l. 9, § 2, eod;—l. 3, § 1, XV., 1;—l. 3, § 12, eod;—l. 6, eod;—l. 7, § 5, eod;—l. 43, eod;—l. 1, § 10, XV., 2;—l. 1, § 1, XV., 3;—l. 2, § 4, XIX., 2;—l. 17, § 12, XXI., 1.

An *actio in factum concepta* could not entail *infamia* when
instituted a year after it had been admissible. Even the
most frequent and most dangerous of all *actiones in factum
conceptae,* the *actio doli,* lost its power of entailing *infamia*
on the defeated defendant after a year. Thus the Roman
jurists had often *two formulae* for such actions as the *actio
depositi,* or *commodati directa,* which brought *infamia* upon
the defendant. One of these *formulae,* the *formula in
factum concepta,* could be used after a year without ruining
the defendant.

We found that the economical disfranchisement of house-
sons was due to the dominant desire to avoid *practical
infamia;* and just as the *actiones in factum* served to
protect against *legal infamia* they likewise served to obviate
the inconvenient consequences of the civil incapacity of
house-sons. *Filiifamilias* had a right to sue with any *actio
in factum concepta,* and their legal incapacity was restricted
to *actiones in jus conceptae.*

The *Interdicta* of Roman Law were likewise originated
by the necessity of obviating the grave consequences of
infamia and correlate institutions; this becomes evident
to whosoever notices the drift of the principle of Roman
Law, to wit: "*Interdictum nullum infamat infamia juris* [k]."

In fact the very rise of the *formulae* in the Roman Law
of procedure is a consequence of that all-pervading desire
to obtain purely civil constructions of jural relations. We
are generally told, on the authority of *Gaius,* that the
ancient mode of procedure by *legis actiones* came into
disuse on account of its extreme formalism. With all
due deference to Gaius and his colleagues I venture to
state, that Roman jurists were most ingenious thinkers
on law, but very poor historians and etymologists indeed.

[k] See l. 13, D (de vi et de vi armata) XLIII., 16. Compare l. 32 D
(de pœnis) XLVIII., 19.

Only a fanatical reverence of antique manuscripts and their authors can blind us to the fact, that the system of *formulae* is immeasurably more complex and subtle than the system of *legis actiones*. The latter, however, offered no shelter against the imminent encroachments and inclemencies of *infamia* and correlate institutions, and consequently it had to be supplanted by a system of greater refinement that could effectively rescue the litigants from civil shipwreck.

/ Even amongst the *in jus conceptae actiones* the *condictiones* were meant to obviate the fatal consequences of *infamia* and correlate institutions : " *Cessat ignominia in condictionibus, quamvis ex famosis causis pendeant,*" says Ulpian [1].

The natural dichotomy of Roman Law is constantly indicated by the Roman terms of *Jus civile* and *Jus honorarium.* The latter was the law of "*Factum ;*" it was not opposed to the former in the sense of a reformer who wants to enforce the truth, that better is the enemy of good : it was its complement. It held the relation of the *interdictum* or the *actio in factum concepta* to the *actio in jus concepta ;* or of *pactum* to *contractus ; possessio* to *dominium ; bonorum possessio* to *legitima hereditas,* &c. This alone explains why Praetorian legislation so seldom ventured on radical reforms, why the XII. Tables continued to be considered living law eight centuries after their promulgation. The *Jus civile* never ceased to be a vital element of Roman Private Law as long as this law really existed ; its rigour and "criminalistic" character was the very leaven of Praetorian legislation and scientific meditations. Roman Private Law means Civil *and* Praetorian Law ; it did not "evolve" out of a victorious struggle of the latter against the former. Just as *homo sui juris*

[1] l. 36 D (de obligationibus et actionibus) XLIV., 7.

and *servus* presuppose and inter-determine one another in indissoluble connection, even so *jus civile* and *jus honorarium.*

Individual Roman jurists had subjective leanings to one division of law in preference to the other. This gave rise to the two famous schools of Roman jurists, the *Proculeiani,* and the *Sabiniani.* The point of difference between these two schools has been a matter of great and learned dispute in Germany and France. It would be uninteresting to rehearse the various opinions, which, as a rule, savor of the dust of learning rather than of the salt of common sense. The fundamental dichotomy of Roman Law seems to almost necessitate the rise of two schools, one of which gravitates towards "*Jus,*" the other towards "*Factum.*"

I said that the dichotomy of Roman Law was a natural product of the peculiar constitution of their commonwealth, and I called attention to the striking similarity between Roman *private* law and modern continental *criminal* law. In fact, to numerous concepts in Roman Law, and more especially in the Roman Law of Procedure, we find close analogies not in the civil but in the criminal law of modern continental nations. Thus the bifurcation of a Roman civil lawsuit in the proceedings *in jure* and *in judicio,*—a bifurcation repeating the general dichotomy of Roman Law in the domain of procedure,—is fairly copied in the criminal procedure of Austria and Germany ; the Roman *litis contestatio* has a nearly faithful copy in one stage of the criminal procedure of the said countries and France ; the theory of evidence in Roman civil lawsuits comes considerably nearer to the theory of evidence in continental trials than in civil suits, &c. For in continental Europe the notion of "social honour" has much of the dreadful character of Roman *infamia,* and although

E

in the majority of cases, where modern social *infamia* is likely to afflict a continental gentleman, the expedient of duelling is resorted to: enough remains to cause the criminal codes of Germany, France, Austria, Italy, &c., to circumscribe crimes and misdemeanors in definitions as carefully worded as were the single syllables of a Roman *formula* in a civil suit, such *formula* being replete with the germs of political ruin, as continental trials are with the germs of social ruin.

DICHOTOMY OF ROMAN PRIVATE LAW.

JUS.	FACTUM.
Homo sui juris	*Homo alieni juris ; servus*
Res mancipi	*Res nec mancipi*
Dominium	*Possessio*
Contractus	*Pactum*
Actio in jus concepta	*Interdictum, actio in factum concepta*
Manus	*Liberum matrimonium*
Hereditas Legitima	*Bonorum possessio*
Proceedings *in jure*	Proceedings *in judicio*

The Two Schools

JUS CIVILE   JUS HONORARIUM

III.

ROMAN LAW, CONTINENTAL GOVERNMENTS, AND MODERN EVOLUTIONIST THEORIES.

Why has Roman Law been adopted in Germany, France, &c., and why not in Hungary, England, and the United States?—Inapplicableness of modern evolutionism to the rise and fall of social institutions, as illustrated by Roman Law.

In our present lecture I am going to discuss two problems, one historical, the other philosophical. The historical problem relates to the influence of Roman Law on modern civilization; the philosophical to the applicableness of modern evolutionist theories to the development of Roman Law.

In the preceding lectures I endeavoured to state the nature of the *vera causa* of Roman Private Law. I contended that Roman Law was the necessary outcome of the *political* constitution of the Roman commonwealth. The bulk of Roman Law owes its existence and character to political forces, and not to economical or social habits and usages. It was the rule of the market, the banker's office, the merchant's shop; but its roots stretched into the political assembly. The bulk of Germanic Law can be sufficiently accounted for by reasons of political economy and finance. Such considerations would help us very little in Roman Law. It was more of a political device

than of an expedient to protect the private rights of individuals. Its main object was to succour the political
integrity of the defendant, and not his financial condition.
As to its *causes,* Roman Law was a product of the political
constitution of Rome. As to its *form,* Roman Law was
a *science.* This circumstance is one of the most momentous
points in the *modern* history of Roman Law. A science is
the result of a strong desire to systematize certain facts.
Facts, as a rule, are extremely refractory and hate to be
reduced to a systematic order under a few general " heads,"
and accordingly some of the simplest facts of the simplest of
all sciences, mathematics, have successfully escaped the lasso
of systematization or " scientification," so to speak ; as, for
instance, the prime-numbers, the law of their sequence being
unknown. But if the desire of people to systematize a
certain cluster of facts be very intense, they generally
manage to so arrange or trim facts as to finally carry their
point.
    So with the facts of *Law.* The facts of Law are, *per se,*
no more willing to submit to the yoke of scientific generalizations, than the facts of fashion, or social conversation.
And with the vast majority of nations, private law is so far
from being the subject-matter of scientific systematization,
that nobody ever attempted to disentangle systematically
the skein of rules that goes to make the private law of those
nations. Thus English Private Law, as well as English
Law of Administration, positively hate generalizations, and
the very first prerequisite of a scientific system, namely,
general definitions, are *rarae aves* in English Common
Law. It is not a mere accidental coincidence, that the
only works on English constitutional and common law, in
which a serious attempt at systematization has been made,
were written by a German, — *Professor Gneist,* — and a
Frenchman,—M. *Glasson,*—these two nations cultivating

the spirit of systematization as a profession. From gaseous aggregates downward they reduce everything to a, b, c, or *a, β, γ*.

From the circumstance, therefore, that the Romans reduced the facts of their law to a science of law, it by no means follows, that law really is just as susceptible of a scientific system, as the facts of plant-life or stone-layers are supposed to be susceptible of being housed in the generalizations of botany and geology. If such were the case; if law as such were susceptible of scientific systematization, Roman Law, being, as it is, the only science of law, could also claim the immense privilege of being the only good and true law, just as we call scientific botany the only true and good botany. And this, no doubt, is the prevalent feeling with the civilians and jurists of the continent. They identify science with truth, and truth with usefulness, just as every body does with regard to mathematical or natural sciences. Consequently they consider Roman Law as the only specimen of private law worthy of that name, and only smile at the incoherent and totally " unscientific pile of precedents," called English or American Common Law.

I am not going to broach the general question whether science is tantamount to truth or merely to a compromise between a number of half-truths : but I am bound to say that the *science* of Private Law is not tantamount to *true* law. The science of Private Law is tantamount to Roman Law. No more. There may be a better law of jural relations between private people ; but there is none other in the form of an equally consistent scientific system.

This very fact is big with the most incisive political consequences. As soon as law becomes the subject-matter of science, and the occupation of professional scientists, it falls entirely out of the hands of the citizens for whom it is destined. Instead of being a popular interest it becomes a class-interest ; instead of being fed by and feeding the popular intellect, it is nursed and pampered in the hothouses of specialist thinkers. No sooner did Roman Law assume its peculiarly scientific features than it left the hearth of the vigorous but untutored *civis*, and withdrew in the chamber of the *jurisconsultus*. Roman law-suits, it is true, were always decided by jurors selected amongst citizens. But a Roman jury was essentially different from a jury in England. In the first place it consisted, as a rule, of one man only. This alone shows that the jury system of Rome did not mean to find the truth of a law-case through the combined efforts of unprofessional citizens. On the contrary, the juror-*judex* was surrounded by a *consilium* of *jurisconsulti*, and he generally took and abided by their advice. Hence the professional jurists of Rome were at once the makers of private law and the judges of particular cases.

Now, if the citizens of a commonwealth give up their direct and immediate influence over the creation and administration of law, they have therewith resigned the better part of their political power. Law, together with the power of convening and directing the popular assembly are the two chief constituents of political liberty. Political liberty means liberty to partake in the making of law and in the deliberations of the Assembly. In modern times, it is true, the sense of real political liberty has been stunned and blunted to such an extent, especially on the continent, that a modern German, for instance, is entirely incapable to grasp the real glory of the legal institutions and works of his free ancestors. Because the law of mediaeval Germany was deposited in disconnected and "unscientific" precedents, called " *Weisthuemer*," and couched in the *naïve* verbiage of folk-books, as the " *Sachsenspiegel*," " *Schwabenspiegel*," and similar compilations : a modern German, perched on the heights of painfully scientific "hand-books" and "text-books" of law, looks down with dis-dain upon the "unsystematic stammerings of his primitive ancestors."

These ancestors, however, if they could see how the law of Germany is completely taken out of the hands of the citizens,—with a slight exception in the administration of criminal law,—would scarcely retain their scornful laughter at a nation that was gullible enough to exchange the inestimable power of making its own law for the gewgaw of so called scientific systematization.

As long as the public life of the Romans gave free scope to the political activity of numerous citizens, the loss of the popular administration of law did not tell very gravely or, at least, not very perceptibly, on the vigour of popular liberty. But when during the first century B. C. the theory and practice of law began to be considered a matter of purely professional nature, that had little or nothing to do with the wishes or opinions of the people, it helped to weaken the failing energy of the other half of political life, and thus speedily led to the establishment of the Empire. For, political institutions derive their vital force not from the wisdom or usefulness they display, but from the in-tensity of interest people vest in them. Wean people from doing their own political business, and they will assent to the establishment of whatever political insti-tutions do not interfere with their private interests.

The political shrewdness of modern rulers, or rather the profoundly adroit advices of their learned counsellors, did not fail to make the best of this remarkable character of Roman Law. Their unique tendency was to bring their subjects under an absolutistic rule, doing all the political business for them, governing them from above. To this end nothing could be more conducive than the introduction

\of Roman Law. The history of this "reception" can be told in a few words.

You will frequently read in German law-books, that the history of the "reception" of Roman Law in Germany—in the course of the fifteenth century—is more or less a profound mystery. You will be told that the "immense historical material" bearing on this point has not yet been duly sifted, and that it will be only after a most laborious study of all the charters, treatises and books of the thirteenth to fifteenth centuries that we shall finally catch a glimpse of the proper historical light to be shed on this puzzle.

The truth of the matter, however, is this, that the learned in Germany, with excessively few exceptions[m] *do not want* to lift the veil off this mystery. It is untrue that the "reception" of Roman Law in Germany is surrounded with such mystery. On the contrary, it is a very simple fact; as simple as the "reception" of the Normans in England. As the latter is a question of military superiority, so the former is of political. In the course of the fifteenth century the innumerable petty rulers of Germany and adjoining countries were on the look-out for effective means how to minimize the political activity of their subjects. One of the devices they applied was the introduction of Roman Law in lieu of the ancient popular law of Germany. *C'est tout.*

Previous to the fifteenth century Germany and the adjoining countries consisted of a vast number of small territories under the government of various princes, civil and ecclesiastical. The dynasties of nearly all the petty and absolutistic rulers of Germany,—whose number even so late as 1803 was no less than 1799, including the "*reichs-*

---

[m] In *Gierke's* "*Genossenschaftsrecht,*" vol. iii. p. 657, Professor *Laband* is said to have pointed out the *political* reasons of the "reception" of Roman Law in Germany.

ritterschaftliche Gebiete"—arose previous to the fifteenth or sixteenth century. But in the period of the Middle Ages they were infinitely less absolutistic than after the Reformation. In the Middle Ages the ordinances and edicts of the territorial princes did not touch upon one hundredth of those subjects regarding which they issued innumerable ordinances in the sixteenth and seventeenth centuries. In fact, the people in Germany, both in country-marks and in territorial cities,—*Landesstaedte*—did a good deal of their own political business. The common law of the country was "found" and administered by the people ; the innumerable "marks" wielded a considerable portion of political power over their members ; the guilds,—*Zuenfte, Gaffel,*—were very far from being the merely commercial unions of France or England, possessing, as they did, a great power of coercion, both political and moral, over their men ; and the free cities of Germany were so many sovereigns.

But this very abundance of innumerable local and disparate polities ; the very fact that the people of Germany were split into countless small "marks" and guilds, and still smaller political corporations, proved fatal to their liberty. Where people are immersed in atomic interests of petty corporations, public-spiritedness is on the wane. But since no country can dispense with the blessings of public-spiritedness, the burghers of Germany were not loth to welcome the constantly increasing meddlesomeness of their rulers. For, this meddlesomeness took the shape of broad public-spiritedness and paternal care for the general welfare. The bulky ordinances—*Landesordnungen* — of German rulers, chiefly in the sixteenth century, form an amazing number of edicts on nearly all affairs of general welfare : on roads and forests, streets and houses, midwives and physicians, waterpipes and chimneys, rivers and mines, manners and ceremonies, &c., &c. In issuing these

ordinances they slowly weaned the people from caring for
their own public welfare, and nothing was more welcome
to the paternal rulers,—*Landesvaeter*,—than a transgression
of one of their innumerable edicts, such a transgression
providing them with the coveted chance to issue *two* new
edicts instead, and thus *in infinitum.*

But while the people of Germany yielded with more or
less grace to the edicts of their rulers on matters of administrative law, they were not equally willing to abandon the
practice of that popular common law which was amongst
their most precious heirlooms descended from hoary
antiquity. In order to put an end to popular law and by
thus exterminating the last vestige of political independence
to reduce their subjects to the condition of minors was the
natural ambition of the rulers. In this they were most
effectively assisted by the scholars of Germany. For
reasons that cannot be discussed here, the whole intellect
of Germany came to be concentrated in the German
Universities. This in itself would not have been very
harmful to the liberty of the people. Unfortunately,
however, the Universities were solely founded by and
dependent on the various rulers of Germany. With the
unimportant exception of the University of *Altorf*, which
was somewhat dependent on the free city of Nuremberg,
not a single free city of Germany founded or endowed a
University. This fact,—never noticed by German historians,
although it had a vast influence on German civilization,—
this fact brought the whole of German intellectual classes
under the immediate sway of the princes. No man could
fill the place of a teacher, clergyman, professor, lawyer or
physician, without taking his degree at one of the Universities of the country. In other words: nobody could earn
his living in one of the intellectual classes without obtain-
ing leave and license from the ruler of the country.

In England the four Inns of Court, for instance, are absolutely independent of the Government. They call members to the bar independently of the pleasure or displeasure of the Government. The English Universities, and chiefly Oxford and Cambridge, are, to all intents and purposes, private corporations. The numerous ministers of dissenting congregations take Holy Orders, and are appointed quite independently of the Government. Hence it is almost impossible for an Englishman to represent to himself clearly and vividly the utter bondage of the intellectual classes of Germany in the sixteenth, seventeenth, and eighteenth centuries, and to a great extent even in the present century. This bondage, by the way, is the chief cause of the fact that the Germans, to the present day, are more interfered with by their twenty-six rulers than any other western country of Europe. For political reforms or revolutions have little hope for lasting success unless the intellectual classes take part in them.

Now, the intellectual classes being, as they were, in the personal service of the rulers, it became a matter of course that everything that could strengthen the power of the ruler would also increase the dignity and standing of his scholars ; and *vice versa.*

The learned university-teachers of Germany took to Roman Law quite naturally. In the first place the study of Roman Law was part of that study of classical antiquity, which to this day has lost nothing of its spell over the minds of students. In the second place it was, as a matter of science, infinitely more satisfactory than the discon nected heaps of single "findings" deposited in the countless precedents of popular law. Thirdly, it afforded an evident chance to secure their exclusive jurisdiction in law-suits. The common people were unable to study or apply the refined rules of Roman Law. On the other

hand, the very clumsiness and unsystematic inconsistency
of all popular law—so similar in the latter respect to the
whimsical irregularity of language — could not compare
favorably with the logical and brief proceedings of Roman
Law. And thus the frequent acts of injustice, unavoidable
in a law, the bulk of which consisted of unaccountable
usage, were so many strong recommendations of the law
of Rome, which seemed to be thoroughly rational and
practical.

Sir Matthew Hale said that the sources of English
Common Law are as unknown as the sources of the Nile.
If that be so, what shall we say of the sources of German
Mediaeval Law? And, in fact, what shall we think of the
systematic order, consistency and practicableness of that
latter law, if we pause for a moment to think of the
well-known shortcomings and very serious blemishes of
English law? Who can satisfactorily explain or account
for the curious bifurcation of English law into common
law and equity? Who can fail to see how frequently
English law confounds civil with criminal, or public with
civil law? Who will seriously defend the colossal costli-
ness of English law-suits? And do not the most fervent
adherents of English law decry its " glorious uncertainty,"
and its excessively casuistical spirit?

If that be the case with the law of modern England,
we need not wonder if the German civilians of the fifteenth
and sixteenth centuries affected or felt a holy horror of the
endless array of inconsistent legal rules and maxims that
went to form the body of German mediaeval common law.
To reduce these countless rules to comprehensive generalizations was impossible, this impossibility being inherent in
popular law, as it is in popular language. To renounce
the desire for generalizations was and is tantamount to
resigning the dignity of a scientific thinker. Thus it

came to pass that *the political ambition of the rulers and the scientific ambition of their professors met in one and the same point.* For, to have general rules of law was the natural desire of the professors in their capacity as thinkers and theoretical teachers; it was likewise the natural desire of the rulers who were intent on nothing more seriously than on levelling down their subjects to uniform *bourgeois* with no difference of legal customs and privileges.

Accordingly the professors hastened to fill ungainly folios with the praises of Roman Law and its purely scientific character. So far they did not overstate their case. Roman Law is thoroughly scientific. But the professors proceeded to say or intimate that Roman Law, being the only scientific law, must needs also be the only true and good law. *Quod non.* But an objection to this fallacy was seldom heard. Who could have raised it? The students and practitioners of Law were hearers of the professors, and, naturally enough, adopted their opinions. The greater the fame of civilians like *Hotomannus, Zasius, Duarenus,* and the two greatest of them, *Cujacius* and *Donellus,* the more it became hopeless to stem a current that was aided by two powers than which there are none greater : political supremacy and intellectual superiority.

Among the great civilians just mentioned are three Frenchmen. All that I have to say with regard to Germany applies literally to France, and I do not hesitate to say, that much as we may personally admire a man like *Cujacius* or *Donellus*—civilians of such colossal grandeur that, beside them, the greatest of modern civilians are dwarfed into comparative insignificance—they and their colleagues in Bourges, Orleans, and Paris, were among the chief causes of the downfall of popular liberty in France. They sapped the foundations of French popular law, rendered it almost useless, thereby weaned the people from doing that important part of their political business, and thus paved the way to constant royal interference. A glance at the history of those countries in Europe that did not adopt Roman Law will prove and illustrate the *political* origin of the "reception" of this law in Germany and France still more forcibly. The Kingdom of Hungary never adopted the theory or practice of Roman Law. This seems all the more strange since Hungary used Latin as the official language of her legislature, laws, and law-courts down to the first quarter of this century. A country so intensely imbued with the idiom of Rome would seem to be quite likely to adopt also the law of Rome. This, however, the Hungarians never did. Their law is essentially similar to the common law of England, in that it is derived mainly from precedents and usage. The unwillingness of the Hungarians to adopt Roman Law was based on a political consideration. Roman Law, they noticed, requires a professional and privileged class of jurists who administer law to the exclusion of all other classes. In German territories the privileged class of civilians were in the service of the rulers. But it so happened that ever since 1526 the ruler, or at least the nominal head of Hungary, was a foreigner : the Archduke of Austria, or Emperor of Germany. Hence to introduce Roman Law in Hungary would have been tantamount to surrendering the law of the country to the administration of foreigners, or of professors, who had a vital interest to work in the interest of their foreign employer, the Archduke of Austria. Consequently the Hungarians prudently abstained from the establishment of numerous Universities, and persistently refused to adopt Roman Law, the scientific excellence of which they otherwise fully acknowledged. For, the Hungarians always were, and to the present moment still are, the only nation on the continent who maintained an amount of political liberty and self-government quite unknown to the rest of continental Europe, particularly in the last two centuries.

The same reason applies to England. England never adopted Roman Law, because it was against the interests of English liberty to confide the making and interpretation of law to the hands of a privileged class of jurists. As said before, Roman Law cannot be adopted unless you adopt a privileged class of professional jurists into the bargain. *The hatred of the English was not so much a hatred of civil law, but of the civilians.* These jurists develop law on the strength of theoretical principles, and actual cases are not decided according to former judgments given in similar cases, but by principles obtained through theoretico-practical speculation. Hence there is no division of questions of law and fact in civil cases; nor is there, in a system of Roman Private Law, any room for juries, and thus law is taken completely out of the hands of the people. This, however, the English would not endure, and thus they naturally fell to confiding their law to their judges. English common law is judge-made law. This alone implies that English common law is naturally casuistical. A judge is not called upon to pronounce on general questions, or show the internal connection of general principles; he is expected to decide a particular case taking into consideration all the alloys of facts and accidental circumstances that, as a rule, clog the pure principle of law. Consequently his decisions do not reveal jural principles in their abstract and clear aspects. This alone, however, would not have prevented English judges from unduly interfering with the law of the country. But in confiding the law of England to them, the English subjoined a fundamental condition, that renders all dangerous class-ambition of their judges in-effective. This condition enjoins the strict observance of precedents. This one rule paralyzes all attempts at a dictatorial supremacy on the part of English judges. While formally allowed to make law, they are practically restricted to merely reveal the law made by their predecessors and by the indirect influence of popular juries.

By a parity of reasoning, the Americans never adopted Roman Law, and even the State of Louisiana, where Roman Law is partly still in force,—the Code Napoleon being part of the common law of Louisiana,—it plays but a subordinate part, and was unable to supersede the use of precedents. So intimately connected with the fundamental political institutions of both England and the United States is the unscientific, atomic, and casuistical character of Anglo-American Law, that all attempts at codifying it have proved futile. The codes of the States of New York, Ohio, &c., have not for one moment retarded the constant increase of precedents, and metaphorically at least, we may say, that these codes form only one more, if bulkier, precedent in the series of their countless predecessors and successors.

Roman Law is a marvellous product of the human mind; its scientific charms are surpassingly great; its simple and practical teachings are most valuable; but the price to be paid for it is too high, it can be obtained only at the expense of a goodly portion of political liberty. As long as the constitutions of England and America remain materially unchanged, Roman Law will never be adopted in its entirety, either in England or the United States, for the simple reason, that Anglo-American jurists are *first* Englishmen or Americans, and *then* jurists.

Investigations into the causes of Roman Law are of very great moment for two reasons: first, on account of the intense interest attaching to the institutions of ancient Rome in general, and to its law in particular; secondly, on account of such investigations being fit to serve as test-cases for the doctrines of modern evolutionism.

The great and signal success of Darwinism in the domain of natural science has filled its adherents with just enthusiasm. The most radical opponent of the theories of Darwin, Haeckel, Huxley, Wallace and other eminent Darwinists cannot but acknowledge that many facts of morphology, botany, zoology and anthropology have been reduced to greater scientific order; and numerous facts hitherto unknown have been discovered through the improved methods of Darwinism. To deny this would be to deny the most evident fact in modern science.

Enthusiasm, however, is likely to carry away its devotees; and, accordingly, the fervent adherents of modern evolutionism were not satisfied with the laurels won in the sciences just named, but essayed to try their victorious concepts on problems that have previously been considered outside the pale of the naturalist. The puzzles of sociology, the enigmas of the rise and development of social institutions, they declared to be amenable to satisfactory solutions by means of ideas and concepts that proved so successful with regard to the physical frame of animals and plants. Religion, marriage-systems, kinship-systems, ceremonies, and laws were and are said to be problems that unbosom their mysteries to "*natural selection,*" "*survival of the fittest,*" "*atavism,*" "*theory of survivals,*" and the rest of Darwinian concepts with astounding willingness. We are taught, that in social institutions, as in animals and animal life, there is an uninterrupted process of evolution going on, one "stage" of civilization succeeding to another "stage,"

F

the "higher" to the "lower," the "heterogeneous" to the "homogeneous;" that humanity was first what the savages of Africa and South America are at present; that by dint of more advanced ideas and greater "enlightenment" social institutions have been slowly improving; and that our present civilization, although containing many "survivals" of ruder and less "enlightened" times, is, by the very working of the principles of "natural selection" and "survival of the fittest," radically superior to the civilizations of either Greece and Rome or the Middle Ages.

While fully acknowledging the great services rendered to natural science by Darwinism, we most positively deny that any one of the great problems of the history of institutions has been brought to a satisfactory solution by means of Darwinian concepts. However, much as we should like to dwell on this most interesting point at full length, we have to restrict ourselves to a more concrete question.

We maintain, that the rise and development of Roman Law, or, to use modern phraseology, that the "evolution" of Roman Law cannot be construed or understood by bringing the concepts of Darwinism to bear upon it. On the contrary: the "evolution" of Roman Law is, as the evolution of all other social institutions, manifest evidence against the applicableness of modern evolutionist concepts to the development of social institutions.

According to evolutionist views the law of a nation is derived either from the law of another nation, or from rudimentary and incipient legal institutions of its own. In both cases one law is derived from another law. This, however, does not hold good in the case of the Romans; the Romans not having derived their law from other nations, nor from an alleged rudimentary law of their own ancestors. That the Romans did not borrow their law from the Greeks or any other nation has been proved nearly two hundred years ago by Vico; that they did not "evolve" their law out of rudimentary "variations," aided by "natural selection in the struggle for life," has been proved, we trust, in these lectures. Roman Law, we said, was an outcome, not of causes pertaining to law, but of causes pertaining to politics. It arose simultaneously with the peculiar constitution of the Roman state. Given the constitution of Rome, the science of Roman Law follows from it *at once:* it is not a matter of slow development, of long growth, of adaptation, or struggle, death, and survival; it is a matter of logical succession. Just as the theorem of Pythagoras follows from the nature of the rectangular triangle at once and irrespective of time: even so the law of Rome from the constitution of Rome. For in fact, the law of Rome was part of Rome's constitution. There is no prior, and no posterior; no antecedent, and no successor. The essential features of Roman Law were extant at the time when the essential features of the Roman republic had come into existence. The rest was mere expansion and elaboration of given principles. But of slow growth, of evolution through stages, there is no trace. The praetorian law, it is true, was immeasurably less developed in the third than in the first century B.C. This, however, was owing not to a lower "stage" in the " evolution " of Roman Law, but to the simple fact that the Romans of the third century did not need an elaborate system of praetorian law, being, as they were, a comparatively small commonwealth.

The evolutionist is in constant demand of enormous periods of time. He believes, that the small and incipient changes, that he is so sorely in need of, are sure to happen in one of the countless minutes of vast infinitudes of time. The incipient "variations"—this the killjoy of Darwinists —he cannot dispense with; at the same time, however, he is unable to assign a definite time to their rise; and thus he drowns his doubts in the extremely plausible assumption, that the required incipient "variation" is more than likely to happen, provided we give it liberal chances of time. Now there is nothing cheaper than abstract time; and each of us is willing to grant any quantity of an object than which nothing is more inexhaustible. So it comes to pass that the vast periods of time demanded from the evolutionist have been willingly granted on all hands.

This may do, and no doubt does in natural science. But it will never do in the science of social institutions. The objects of the latter are distinctly and well-nigh essentially different from those of the former, in that they invariably refer to organized *aggregates* of individuals; whereas biology proper treats, as a rule, of individuals only. One fox does and acts exactly what a thousand foxes are doing and acting. The actions performed by one man, on the other hand, are totally different from the actions of organized aggregates of a thousand men. *Sociology treats of aggregates of individuals, institutions being the outcome of the activity of aggregates.* In large aggregates, however, movements are much less given to unaccountable changes, to chance "variations." No stretch of time will give us a right to assume the rise of such incipient "variations," as Darwinists constantly presuppose, declaring at the same time, that the laws of "variations" are covered with "profound mystery." Instead of begging incipient "variations," and leaving the explanation of their rise entirely unattempted, the *student of institutions has to insist on nothing more uncompromisingly, than on the explanation of what Darwinists call "variations."*

In other words: Darwinists constantly beg incipient "variations," waiving at the same time all responsibility of accounting for such " variations." The student of social institutions never begs incipient " variations ;" he asks for such variations only as he can sufficiently account for.

Hence, the methods of Darwinism desert the investigator of social institutions at the very point where his investigations commence. In other words, they do not assist him at all, proving, as they do, inapplicable to sociological problems.

Roman Law offers, as we saw, the " variation " of a civil law saturated with elements of Criminal Law. The causes of this variation are perfectly clear to the careful student of Roman institutions. It was the necessary check of a constitution that was built and erected on the strict morality of a few citizens. The question again as to the causes of this restriction to a few citizens resolves itself, as we shall see in the next lecture, into the problem of the causes of Roman slavery, which in its turn reposes on the fact that the Graeco-Roman age knew of no other civilization than a city-state civilization. This fact again arose from the geographical position of antique classical countries, all of them being situated on the shores of the Mediterranean sea.

Thus we can follow up the concatenation of causes under the constant and benignant light of clear ideas, until we reach causes the explanation of which devolves upon another description of thinkers. But nowhere did we say that " variations " are to be begged, are to be supposed to crop up as mere chance rovers in the boundless expanse of infinite time.

Nor did we see that the " variation " of law, called Roman Law, was kept up, augmented, fortified and rendered more useful in the " struggle for life " by the forces of " natural selection," or " sexual selection," or " survival of the fittest." The " variation" of Roman Law was in need of no such forces ; it was born full-fledged, irresistible from the very beginning. It was not the result of an alleged struggle of the Praetorian system against the old system of *jus civile;* on the contrary, these two systems were mutually interdependent and affiliated throughout all periods of Roman history.

Nor can we perceive any "survivals" in Roman Law. Our view of institutions being that all *present* institutions are kept in existence by *present* causes : we cannot adopt the evolutionist views of "survivals." Odd habits and ceremonies of our age, for instance, that are commonly explained on the assumption of their being "survivals" of former ages, can all be accounted for by the working of present, *if latent*, causes. This is likewise the case with similar habits and apparent oddities in Roman Law. In Professor Ihering's "Spirit of Roman Law" a considerable number of such "survivals" are enumerated; the theory of "survivals," however, is not drawn upon, and the great civilian rightly remarks : "On pourrait certes soutenir que la force d'inertie, la puissance de l'habitude seules en ont fait une forme : mais *il ne faut pas oublier que la puissance de l'habitude à elle seule suppose déjà une disposition subjective favorable à la forme* [n]."

Evolutionist theories finally draw most heavily on death. Death is the great friend of theories that have to do away with innumerable inconvenient individuals, in order to make room for such as prove fitted for the "sweet habit of existence." But what is the meaning of death with regard to social institutions? What can death mean for aggregates, the members of which are constantly regenerated from the inexhaustible fountain of life? Aggregates of people do not die like individuals. They have a life of considerably more tenacious cast. They sometimes last for thousands of years, as in the case of the orthodox Jews,

[n] *R. von Ihering*, "L'Esprit du Droit Romain" (French transl., Paris, 1880), vol. iii. pp. 195, 196.

the Chinese, and many other nations. Institutions eman-
ating from and grafted upon such aggregates are not like
the colours or limbs of animals. They are based upon
common ideas, and many ideas contain the germ of eternity. Men in their quality as members of aggregates do
not struggle for physical and ephemeral life alone. They
struggle for another life also; nay their noblest and highest
efforts are directed towards a life beyond the limits of mere
countable days and nights. The base of their aspirations
thus being shifted from the narrow plane of divisible time
to the boundless ranges of eternity : what can a doctrine
avail us that creeps along the lowly fences of months
and years, and registers the deaths of single individuals?
Nations do not live in the jail of time ; they live or try
to live in the open grounds of eternity. Instead of wishing
for the death of the unfit, they frequently so arrange
matters as to care for nobody as lovingly as for the very
people who are unfit for the struggle of life. And, *vice
versa ;* nations frequently pay the highest modes of worship
to the very individuals that died an early death in the service of ideas maintaining the commonwealth of that nation.
In what sense of the word can we say that Cæsar died?
Was the effect of his actions, words, and writings lost like
that of a dead fox? Could the bearing of every minute
of his life on the Roman commonwealth be effaced by that
accident on the Ides of March, 44 B.C., that mortals call
the death of Cæsar ? Nay, can the effect of the life of the
least and most insignificant Roman be said to have van-
ished at all ? Was not Rome the product of the Romans,
and does not Rome still govern the world, or two thirds
of it ?

Whatever death may mean in animals—and a late theory
pronounces death on Death with regard to earlier periods,
contending that death has been " evolved," like all other

biological facts, in course of time—it means nothing or very little in the history of aggregates of people. Hence the great fuss made over death by evolutionists is but an uncouth racket for the student of institutions. He does not draw on death; he does not think that the span of life enjoyed by an individual is typical for the life lived by aggregates. Aggregates rise and decay according to rules totally different from the rules of life in force among animals and plants. They live in a temporal space beyond mere phenomenal Time; and if the patient and careful student of the rise, development, and decay of Roman Law, or any other social institution, cannot but feel a profound antipathy against the teachings of modern evolutionists, he does so mainly because he is fully convinced, that the life of nations is based not on the passing waves of Time, but on the unchanging expanse of Eternity.

IV.

THE CLASSICAL CITY-STATE.

Its influence on : Slavery — Position of Women — Private Life— Religion — Downfall of the Roman Empire — Development of Christianity.

OF all the nations of antiquity that have influenced the course and direction of mediaeval and modern civilization none can rival the Greeks and Romans. Their institutions form the subject-matter of some of our most engaging studies. Although our sources of knowledge regarding the true nature of Greek and Roman institutions are far from complete, and although the bulk of these sources has been studied and re-studied by innumerable scholars, yet every year brings fresh testimony to the ardour with which these studies are still pursued, and, as it were, constantly recommenced, as if they had never been attempted by hosts of predecessors. Times considerably nearer to us are studied with less enthusiastic zeal ; and the minds of the European and American youths are systematically trained to an ever-growing interest in the history and institutions of Greece and Rome.

Has this very extensive study of Latin and Greek authors, inscriptions, monuments and coins been productive of a corresponding wealth of clear and precise ideas about the institutions of Greece and Rome ? Do we generally possess as clear an idea of the social or political institutions of Athens or Rome as of some of our own country? Can we understand, for instance, the influence of Greek oracles as clearly as the influence of the modern press? Or can we bring home to our mind the causes of the marvellous variety of commonwealths in Greece as contrasted with the striking uniformity of commonwealths in Italy? Can we thoroughly understand the puzzles of Graeco-Roman polytheism, a creed where gods were allowed to indulge in crimes and dissipations that would have been most gravely resented in the adorers of such gods? Do we know the practical causes of classical slavery, a slavery so distinctively different from modern modes of bondage? Or can we represent to ourselves the working causes that brought about the curious position of Greek women, or that of Roman matrons more curious still? By putting these questions, I mean to ask whether we possess a practical knowledge of the solution of these problems. And by practical knowledge I mean a knowledge that does not consist in learned quotations from authors only.

Authorities are indispensable, true enough. But authorities alone will seldom help us to get at that practical knowledge of Greek or Roman institutions, which alone deserves the name of real knowledge. We have to go *beyond* our authorities. He who flatters himself to understand a Greek or Roman institution will find a sure and most effective test of his knowledge by putting to himself the following two kinds of questions : (1) what corresponds to this or that Greek or Roman institution in our own institutions? take e.g., the Roman Censor or Tribune. What corresponds, entirely or partially, to the Roman Censor or Tribune in English or American institutions? Or, is there a modern institution that corresponds, entirely or partly, to Greek oracles? (2) Why did the Romans or Greeks not possess such or such an institution, that seemed to be in

keeping with their social or political frame? e.g., Why did
the Romans *never* think of a representative government,
except in the case of provincial diets? why did the Romans
not practice the custom of duels? why did the Greeks *not*
cultivate the Science of Private Law? why did the Greeks
not institute gladiatorial games? To these and similar
questions the ancient authorities cannot furnish us an
answer; the ancients could not have known our civilization,
and thus neither comparison to ours nor negative questions
concerning theirs could have occurred to them. But unless
you can answer such and similar questions you cannot say,
that you thoroughly construed and understood an institution of the past. It is therefore with a view to this, the
real principle of historical knowledge, that I am going to
discuss a few of the leading facts of Graeco-Roman civilization, comparing or contrasting them to their modern counterparts. You may, of course, object, that the assumption
of such counterparts presupposes that History constantly
repeats itself, that the later generations do not evolve new
and unprecedented forms, and that evolution has no
meaning in human history. In saying so you have said
exactly and precisely what I hold to be the case, and
accordingly I most heartily subscribe the opinion of the
great scolder of mankind, of Schopenhauer, that he who has
read Herodotus has read all history, the rest being variations on an old theme.

As I occasionally remarked in one of our former lectures,
the most fundamental and general fact in Graeco-Roman
civilization is its being exclusively a city-civilization. The
domicile of a nation is one of the silent, slow and unosten-
tatious causes that bear upon the cast of the nation's whole
civilization much more powerfully than many a louder and
more conspicuous influence. A nation living in tents, or
straggling houses over wide meadows, or in common

houses, like some of the ancient pueblos in America, who had one gigantic house for hundreds of members of one family, or in boats, or in islands, undergoes vast influences by the very mode of its habitations. Country-life in its modern form, that is, village-life, is the fertile cause of peculiar institutions. Look at modern Europe and America. What we are pleased to call European civilization *par excellence*, or, in other words, Western civilization, is characterized mainly by the vast preponderance of urban over village life. In the East of Europe, in Russia, Roumania, Hungary, Servia, &c., village-life preponderates enormously. In America, on the other hand, where nothing will surprise the traveller more than the high average intelligence of every single American, every American speaking United States, as they call English, with remarkable purity and absence of provincialism or false suffixes or affixes,—in America there is practically speaking no village-life at all; all Americans live in cities, that is in places with urban customs and institutions. The intimate contact of city life brings about an infinitely increased intensity of mental and emotional actions and reactions, and thereby a more rapid growth of thoughts and activities of all kind. If we now apply this to Greece and Rome, we shall easily comprehend, that the astounding intellectual power manifested in those common-wealths was mainly due to the fact, that living as they did exclusively in cities, their intellect had to undergo more powerful incitements than the intellect of nations whose members live in loose contact with one another. The Samnites in Italy, the Acarnanians in Greece are examples of nations who did not live in cities exclusively, and we all know that they were renowned for military valor but insignificant as far as civilization is concerned. Greeks and Romans were, on the whole, exclusively city-nations; that is, the whole of the population was concentrated, as it were, in one city. You cannot lay sufficient stress on this one fact; for this one fact together with very few other facts of equal generality goes to make the fundamental layer of the gigantic fabric of classical civilization.

Let us try to represent to ourselves the difficulties of the social and political problem involved in the fact of a whole nation being domiciled in one and the same city. The Americans, as I said a few moments ago, have to face the same problem; and in their case the problem is even somewhat aggravated. For according to their constitution every single citizen shall enjoy the same amount of political franchise. But while the political rights or powers accorded to every citizen are, and can be, kept upon a level, the economical rights and powers cannot be kept in a state of equality. There are poor and rich citizens in America just as well as everywhere else; and the poorer people by far outnumber the wealthy members. If, therefore, the government of cities should be entrusted to the inhabitants themselves, the poorer voters, who always command the majority, would soon run the city treasury into colossal debts for the sake of giving occupation to the poor, or of granting loans at very easy terms.

This is one, and only one, of the many and inevitable difficulties in which city governments are sure to be entangled, if universal suffrage entitles every citizen to a vote in matters of city government. What are the Americans doing to obviate such colossal abuses? They totally disfranchise their city governments, and shift the right of settling important matters of city administration from the city to the state-assembly. As a mere fact American cities have much less municipal liberty than Russian cities. *There is no American citizenship proper, or " freedom."* The extreme difficulty of city-states is also most vividly

illustrated by the history of the cities of Italy in the
Middle Ages. With the single and singular exception
of Venice they continued to be in constant internal up-
roar. They never knew how to adjust the conflicting
claims of their citizens, and thus one noble family or
another could temporarily exercise an almost tyrannical
supremacy by dexterously eluding the various parties.

The Greeks and Romans were placed before the same
difficulty. Their states were exclusively city-states ; they
had no higher political organism that could have played
the part of the mediator, as does the American State proper,
and the Union. It is thus self-evident that all the dangers
of a city-government, in which every citizen has a right
to exercise political influence, threatened the very existence
of the classical commonwealth. In addition to this, the
internal cause of imminent danger, there was the equally
grave danger of the animosity and bellicose temper of every
surrounding city-state. But there also was a third source,
and perhaps a still more awful source of apprehension.
Suppose a Roman citizen living in the fourth or fifth century
before Christ finds one day, on sober reflection over his lot,
that the constant warfare of Rome completely shattered his
fortune, his health, and reduced him to most aggravating
straits. A few miles from Rome were cities that happened
to prosper. Why should he not go and try his fortune in
one of those neighbouring places ? Hundreds of thousands
of emigrants think the same way in our time, and undertake journeys infinitely more expensive and troublesome
than the journey that a Roman would have had to
undertake. Why, then, did he *not* undertake it ? Why
did he rather suffer the merciless law of his city to dis-
perse all his goods, and why did he not emigrate to Veji
or some other neighbouring city ? Religion, race, and all
other causes that are so frequently referred to whenever

we do not know how to discover the actual causes of historical events, will help us here very little. The religion and race and language of the Italian tribes and nations were nearly alike.

But there was another reason. Every city-state was naturally aware of this great danger of losing large numbers of its citizens by emigration. Now in order to increase the value of citizenship they endowed it with numerous emoluments of a very material character, and heightened its value by narrowing the possibilities to become a citizen of the state. In our own times citizenship is a right of rather pale and lifeless complexion. When the Germans conquered Alsace and Lorraine they never for a moment thought of *not* conferring the right of citizenship on the population of the two provinces. To be naturalized in any of the modern countries requires mostly the payment of a certain sum of money, and in some American States, as in Indiana, Colorado, Kansas, Michigan, Minnesota, &c., a sojourn of half a year or less, together with a "declared intention," is sufficient. A classical city-state never dreamed of conferring its citizenship on conquered states. This would have surely diminished the value of this precious right. Just think of the contrast of the so-called social war of ancient Italy (90 B.C.) and a modern war! The majority of Italian nations rushed to arms against Rome, because Rome did not choose to grant them the Roman franchise. To our modern ideas this seems to be quite ridiculous. Think of Switzerland making war on France because France does not want to embody Switzerland into the territory of the .French Republic. Does this not seem like forcing somebody at the point of a revolver to accept £1,000 a year? But for the reason just mentioned the classical city-state had a vital interest to so increase

the value of its franchise that emigration or desertion
became entirely useless.

Now this very tendency to increase the value of citizenship could evidently not be realized in a more effective
way than by minimising the number of persons who had
access to the city-franchise. Hence a necessity arose to
disfranchise, or rather not to admit to the franchise, a large
number of people in order to thus intensify the value
set upon the city-franchise, which, in its turn, was the
only safeguard against the dissolution of classical city-
states. Just as the Romans could not be persuaded amicably
to grant the Roman franchise to their Italian allies, and
much less to their provincials : even so, and for the very
same reason, the citizens of classical city-states in general
were obliged, and by dint of the most irresistible reasons of
self-preservation, to disfranchise large numbers of people
living in their cities, and to carry this disfranchisement
the farther the more valuable the franchise became. In
other words, they had to deprive aggregates of people of
their political status ; or still shorter, *they had to make
them slaves.* And this I take to be the real and actual
cause of classical slavery.

Classical slavery was not the outcome of an inferior
degree of morality, nor an offshoot of a civilization of a
lower type of growths ; the Greeks and Romans were
fully aware of the unnaturalness and cruelty of slavery as
such. You can easily fill pages with quotations from
classical writers showing how sensible they were of the
ethical and social evils of slavery. And to give one
striking, if indirect, proof, let me refer to the well-established
fact, that Christianity, the very life-spirit of which seems to
condemn slavery, and in the name of which the humane
diplomates of our time, for instance, the meek and good

Bismarck, send armies to Africa for the extinction of slavery in Zanzibar,—I say the Christian fathers never so much as broached the question of the abolition of slavery. On the contrary : fully aware of the inevitableness of the institution they exhorted the slaves to obedience, and as we all know, St. Paul himself had a slave and never thought of emancipating him. Classical slavery was a necessary product of the enormous value set upon political franchise ; and this value, in its turn, was a necessary product of the fact, that the ancients did not know of any other form of Commonwealths, than single city-states. The cause of this latter fact I shall have the honour of discussing at some future time.

You remember that remarkable passage in Aristotle's Politics, a work more important to the student of history and politics than Euclid is to the geometrician, where Aristotle tries to forecast the modern state, the territorial state. It occurs towards the end of the fifth chapter of the third book (the last 4 §§). He comes to the conclusion, that such a state is no state at all. And in fact, for the ancients there was no state but a city-state, and consequently Aristotle was perfectly right in declaring that slavery is a matter of course.

In the antique state to abolish slavery was tantamount to abolish the state itself, tantamount to complete annihilation of the then only possible *manière de vivre.* It is puerile to speak of Aristotle, the author of the profoundest ethical writings, as of a benighted heathen with regard to the question of slavery. He considers slavery, *classical* slavery, as a matter of course ; and so did the Christian teachers of the first three centuries. He does not denounce it ; but does Origen, Tertullian, or Irenaeus do so ? Let us be just ; nay, let us be modest. Before taunting one of those giants of mind, we had better patiently investigate the

question, and in the end we shall find that, while it may not
suit our palates, yet we have to concede, that classical
slavery was a matter of course, and the premium for that
astounding exuberance of political and intellectual products
that we call classical antiquity, and without which our
mental food would lack the better part of its force. To
decry classical slavery on the one hand, and to revel in
Homer, Sophocles, Sappho, or the sculpture and architecture
of Greece, or derive constant edification and enthusiasm
from the study of Roman history, on the other hand, is an
ugly piece of unfairness. Who ever respected the fortunate
heir of millions that reviled the man whose money he so
lavishly enjoys? I am no defender of slavery, Heaven
forbid ; but when I see that certain nations, under the
pressure of causes beyond their control, are forced to disfranchise large portions of their fellow-beings : I think, that
instead of indulging in self-complacent conceit and pride
over our own goodness and greatness, and instead of
reviling those nations, we had better thank our destiny
that we are not under a similar pressure and can afford to
be liberal and humane.

It is the same case with the position of women in Greece
and Rome. In some classical commonwealths, e. g. in
Athens, legitimate wives were kept in strictest seclusion ;
and for the very same reason that I adduced for the institution of classical slavery. The Athenian franchise
was so exceedingly valuable, financially, socially, and
politically, that the question of legitimate birth ·was a
question of infinitely higher importance than, e.g., now-a-
days. Accordingly, house-wives were kept confined to their
houses so that the slightest doubt of illegitimacy could
not be cast upon the offsprings of a citizen ; they could
not even go to the theatre, or appear without escort in the
streets, &c. In Sparta, on the other hand, women enjoyed

a freedom, for which the advanced ladies of our blessed times could entertain some envy. The question of legitimacy was also of great moment; but the seclusion that in Athens was entailed upon wives, was, in Sparta, practised against foreigners, and so the danger of the irruption of undue elements was obviated.

In Rome women were for centuries so completely in the power of their husbands that they were considered as their daughters, and sons could call their mother their sister. The highly dignified position of a Roman housewife was, however, quite independent of this, the merely legal and political aspect of the matter. Their apparent subjection to their husbands was due to the same causes that produced the disfranchisement of slaves, and they gladly abstained from enjoying ampler rights in the face of the glory reflected upon them from the splendour of their fathers, husbands, and sons. To revolt against their inferior position would have been to tarnish the splendour of those they loved best. If, therefore, the noble virgins and matrons of Rome, and the beautiful maidens and wives of Athens did not think of shaking off some of the shackles that seem to be so unbearable to the fair sex of our own days, they did so not on account of an inferior intellect or for lack of education, but because the peculiar grandeur of their fathers, husbands, and sons required such a self-sacrifice. Women after all have only one main vocation—love; and this the Greek and Roman women faithfully fufilled. In our own days, when the political and social grandeur and splendour of the male individual has been dwarfed into pigmy shape, displaying the sallow complexion of an impoverished organism, in our days the ladies rightly feel that a change ought to be brought about—and we all know they vigorously proceed in achieving it. Luck to all their enterprises—but please do not look down upon the sweet and intensely sympathetic figure of the antique woman who cheerfully retired into the shadow of her household, in order that her dearest ones may enjoy a development, both physical and mental, than which the world has seen none greater.

This retiring position of women brought about a re-markable feature of classical civilization — *the lack of private life.* Private life proper did not exist in Graeco-Roman times previous to the rise of Christianity, and not to a great extent in the first three centuries of our era. For private life cannot develop without women occupying a prominent position in it. The charms of private life are mainly the charms of social contact with women. But where public life is so intensely developed as it was in Greece and Rome, there private life has few chances of existence. Public and private life are com-plementary; they supplement one another. Wherever the arts and amusements of private life are carried to a high degree of perfection there public life must needs be on the wane; and *vice versa.* At the times of absolutism in con-tinental countries of Europe, that is, at the times when the people did practically never meddle with or take part in the transaction of political business, their private life was evolving charms and attractions of the most captivating kind. It is no exaggeration to say that the Vienna valse has proved one of the strongest pillars of the Austrian dynasty. People so passionately fond of dancing are naturally averse to the practice of dry and prosaic politics, and thus the reigning dynasty has free scope. The same remark applies to modern France, into which a vigorous spirit of self-relying popular politics will be breathed only when Frenchmen will cease to be so enamored of their marvellous theatres, concerts, *salons*, and other amusements generally. Private life in Rome was a small world of its own, poorly developed—remember the frequent complaints of Cicero about the total lack of congenial society; the Romans had no private games like our cards or chess, and those that they had were insignificant beside their gigantic public games, where 30,000 to 40,000 people attended blood-curdling shows. It is but a matter of course, that no person will spend much time with private games when he can enjoy the thrilling excitements of the Roman circus, or the majestic spectacle of Olympian games, Attic theatres, forensic orations, public lectures of Greek philosophers, and similar grand amusements.

The classical state being built on the public-spiritedness of a comparatively small number of men, it was a mere matter of course, that these few men had to devote all their power of mind and character to the business of the State, that is to say, they had to forego the pleasure of being private men. The greatest writers of Rome were to a greater or lesser extent statesmen, or men engaged in public life, and many of them were writers only incidentally, like Cicero and Caesar, and with few exceptions, their writings are not very extensive—they lacked the broad leisure of modern private men who, retiring from all public life, throw out ponderous volumes by the score. In fact, we can state it broadly that classical antiquity did not know the phenomenon of private individuality, and that is, by the way, one of the reasons why classical writings do not appeal to us on a first reading, we being intensely private individuals.

This marked discrepancy manifests itself most forcibly in the *religion* of the ancients. There is a striking contrast between the religion of the ancients and modern creeds. While extremely anxious to regard and handle all concerns of the state in a public way, by means of *public* meetings and *general* decisions, the ancients left

the practice of religion mainly in the hands of the single
families. Now-a-days we find it quite natural that people
unite in public and common prayers, instead of each house-
father officiating privately to his folks. Domestic religious
service has been reduced to a few short prayers and
benedictions. In classical antiquity domestic religious
service played a *rôle* equal if not superior to the public
service. We go to church as the natural meeting-place
for religious ceremonies. The classical temple, on the
other hand, was not the meeting-place of the congregation.
It was the abode of the deity; nothing more. The
domestic religious service had an abundance of development; it varied almost from family to family, and the
uniformness of ceremonies in any one of our modern per-
suasions did not exist. In other words: we are more public-
spirited, as it were, in religious institutions than the
ancients. In their public religion they disregarded the
metaphysical cravings of the individual, and this was in
perfect keeping with their State-organism. The individual
soon gets aware of his mortality, and naturally enough looks
for comfort and solace regarding after life and superhuman
issues. The state as such is callous to such queries; the
state is immortal, and after-life has no meaning for it.
Hence the public religion of the ancients, or the religion of
the state, totally discarded and ignored those points that
form the very soul of modern creeds. Instead of rearing its
religious edifice on the ethical and strictly religious emotions
of individual man, the antique city-state built up its religion
according to the principles which it practised in the construction of its public buildings. This principle was, as we
all know, the principle of grand beauty. Classical religion,
classical public religion, was a religion of the beautiful, a
divinification of beauty in all the manifold manifestations
of that ideal power. Beauty commands admiration; beauty

has a direct, immediate and elementary power over the emotions of people, and it is easily turned to public purposes. The ancients lacking the depth of individual private life were deficient in sympathy with the inner life of religious edification.

Public life is, on the whole, naturally more cheerful and hopeful than private life, and thus people spending nearly all their lives in public pursuits were averse to gloomy and austere religious ceremonies, and readily united in the adoration of a power that will to the end of humanity continue to brighten up and cheer the minds of men. Beauty, if we really acquire a genuine and appreciative sense of its glory, can be properly called a divine principle, and the intense attachment of classical citizens to their statues of gods, temples, and public buildings will be easily understood by whosoever has learned to feel the transcendent beauty of the remains of antique sculpture and architecture. There are cases on record that certain city-states of the ancients endured the extreme vicissitudes of a protracted siege rather than surrender their beautiful statues of gods to their enemies. Even in our machine-stricken times we may notice that nations living mainly in the streets, market-places, and other public localities, as the Italians and French, soon acquire a personal grace of gestures which will never fail of enchanting the unprejudiced observer. In Graeco-Roman times, when public life was, so to speak, the only life, grace and beauty so thoroughly permeated the whole of the commonwealth that it became one of its domineering principles. The Greeks and Romans, but chiefly the Greeks, were the real inventors of beauty; they first brought it to life, and stamped upon it the mark of an eternal principle. This being the case, and nations generally deifying those principles by force of which they exist, it is no wonder that the ancients finally

arrived at the point of making a religion of what formed
one of the main elements of their life.

Wherever we turn in our historical investigations of
Graeco-Roman institutions we can trace the workings and
bearings of that all-powerful fact in the antique civilization,
to wit, that it was an exclusive city-civilization. If we
were to characterize modern and mediaeval civilization by
their main features, we could content ourselves with pointing out, that modern civilization is not an exclusive city-
civilization. This one fundamental fact sheds light on the
majority of ancient and modern institutions. The city-civilization of the ancients necessitated the disfranchisement
of the majority of men and women; it caused their
exclusive public life, and was at the bottom of all their
political and religious institutions. And this circumstance
alone suffices to indicate the causes of the downfall
of classical commonwealths. A civilization grafted on
city-states is not commensurate with enormous territorial
expanse. It requires small territories. As soon as
the Roman Empire assumed dimensions far exceeding
the limits of Italy or Greece, its institutions, meant as
they were for a small city-state, lost their vital power.
The vast majority of their subjects became indifferent
to a state that ignored their ambition and capacity. A
Roman province was ruled by an excessively small number
of Roman officials ; few provincials, therefore, if any, had
a chance to become members of government. Nothing
promoted the Byzantine Empire so efficaciously as the
elaborate net of administrative offices which they cast over
every single one of their provinces. These offices were
filled with ambitious people from the provinces who thus
felt attached to the reigning dynasty with bonds of strong
interest. The early emperors did not change materially
the republican system of provincial administration, and

this system, while working most admirably and effectively, slowly weaned the bulk of the population from taking any lively interest in the existence of an empire that took no notice of them. So that the real cause of the downfall of antique civilization has to be found in the anomaly of the enormous extent of an empire the institutions of which were not meant for large territories with over 100,000,000 people. The military success of the Romans produced the unification of vast territories and an enormous multitude of people under *one* head ; their institutions were sufficient to rule this multitude, but not adequate to fill them with a strong interest in the existence of this Empire. And so the Empire collapsed.

We can frequently hear of the extreme depravity of the late Romans, of their dissolute mode of life, and of all kinds of ungodly things that they are said to have perpetrated, as the cause of their downfall. I am not going to assert that the later Romans or Greeks were model types of moral perfection. But who has the courage to assert that any of the modern nations harbours a smaller amount of vice and evils ? The ancients had the courage of their vices, and, in their writings, talked very plain language indeed. But if we rake together a lot of offensive stories from Martial or Juvenal, or other professional satirists, thinking that such stories are sufficient evidence for the general depravity of Rome—and, as you are aware, the learned work of Professor *Friedländer*, for instance, abounds in such kind of evidence,—we do the ancients most grievous injustice. Who will judge a nation by the writings of professional satirists ? And if the Romans were so utterly depraved, how was it that so many amongst them felt disposed at the very rise of Christianity to accept the heavy duties of that creed, a religion than which we know none purer or more sublime ? No, let us discard all school-declamations against the moral degeneracy of the Romans being the cause of the downfall of the Empire. That Empire decayed, or rather changed its frame, because of its inability to engage a strong interest of its subjects in its further existence. The qualities of a Roman or Greek citizen necessary for the maintenance of the classical city-state were so high-strung, they taxed the moral and mental faculties so highly, that large masses of people could not be expected to possess them; and they did not possess them, and so the Roman Empire fell to the ground. This circumstance ought never to be lost sight of when we compare antique with modern civilization.

The ancients did not do as many things as we do; but the few they did they did more perfectly. We have more people enjoying political franchise; but where are those overtowering individuals of the ancients who combined in *one* magnificent soul the forces of ten great moderns? What a fuss do people make over Bismarck,—one might think the Montblanc or the Chimborazo has donned human forms and stalks amongst the living! But what then shall we say of Julius Caesar, who was Bismarck, General Moltke, and the historian Macaulay in one person? What of Alexander? what of Aristotle? We moderns have more sciences; but how many of our sciences have the finish of Greek geometry or Roman Law? We have more lyrical poets, to be sure; but how many thousands of lyrical volumes would we give for one poem of Sappho's? I am not going to push this line of thought to its extreme point. I have only to say, that if one tenth of what *we* are doing, thinking, and composing will excite so much attention in 2,000 years hence, as does all and everything that the Greeks and Romans have done 2,000 years ago, we may congratulate ourselves most heartily indeed.

And to come to the final point of our survey. The

eternal value of Graeco-Roman civilization rests also on
the fact of its having been one of the main factors of the
rise and growth of that institution which to the present
day is the foundation of both our public and private life—
I mean *Christianity.* Let me premise a general statement,
in order to be on clear terms with every single lady and
gentleman who honour me to-night with their presence :
I do believe in a divine origin of Christianity ; I add :
I do believe in a divine origin of all institutions of mankind. Their roots extend into the realm of that power
that all of us are agreed to call divine. When, therefore,
I shall try to trace the connection of the rise of Christianity with events of a mundane character, I shall do
so simply to show this connection, but not with a tendency to impress the belief that this connection alone
suffices to account for the rise and growth of Christianity.
The most determined orthodox cannot fail to recognize
that Christianity arose in the Roman Empire. Hence
it is a legitimate question : What is the connection of
Graeco-Roman with Christian institutions? How far did
Graeco-Roman institutions influence the growth of Christianity? Or to give the problem a more concrete form :
Given the condition, political and social, of the Roman
Empire in the first century, how did it act upon the growth
of Christianity? We all know that in the first century of
our era many a high-minded thinker and reformer tried
to recast the frame of society and to turn the minds of
people into new channels of thought. Such a mind, e.g.,
was Apollonius of Tyana. Why did none of them succeed? Why was it that of all these reformers, Christian
teachers alone succeeded? If we satisfy ourselves with
referring the success of Christian teachers to the divine
truth contained in their teachings, we fail to understand
why this success came about so very slowly and with such

enormous effort. The Christian teachers did not attempt to alter the social frame of the then society. Modern Socialism avowedly intends doing away with existing social institutions, with aristocracy, peasantry, &c. The first Christian teachers, as I remarked a few moments ago, never attempted to abolish any of the main social institutions of the Roman Empire, not slavery, not Roman citizenship, not Roman Law. And yet it cannot be denied that Christianity wrought deep changes in the social fabric of the Empire. Which, then, was the point of attack that gave to Christian teachers such enormous leverage?

The Roman Empire sinned chiefly in that it did not employ women and the majority of men in pursuits of interests of a higher order. Men do crave for the ideal. In the long run people will not be satisfied with the machine-like routine of every-day life without satisfying their higher aspirations. But you will ask me, why was it that women and the majority of men were so long content with living an insignificant life? Why was it that those women and men did not aspire to a higher position *before* the first century of our era? To this there is a very simple answer : By the first century of our era the legislation of Rome had loosened the fetters of women, and of men in bondage, to a very considerable extent. Women, housewives, were no longer kept in the strict seclusion of former centuries, and the absolute rights of ownership, the right of use and *abuse* in slaves, was toned down to a human right. The next consequence of this was that women began to assert their rights as individuals. They desired to play some *rôle* in the actual world of Rome. But this world had no place for women. Antique civilization was not only a city-civilization, but an exclusive male civilization. No sooner were laws issued that did away with the retired position of women, than the women, like all newly emancipated people, strove to be given a more prominent part in the commonwealth. This desire was more than amply satisfied by Christianity. In Christian communities women played a very important part; a Christian woman was essentially different from a heathen woman. She attended the frequent public church-meetings of men; she was expected to exhort, to teach her husband and her family. This increased importance of women was a great factor in the general development of Christianity.

But a still greater factor was the adoption of that political organization, which the Romans had matured into a system of most effective force. The system of government as practised by the Romans was most carefully imitated by the Christian bishops and priests. The very office of bishops was a close imitation of those Roman provincial *curatores* that combined financial and political functions. But the Church instead of excluding the bulk of the people from the government, as did the Romans, did not omit to place the commonwealth of the Church on a purely democratical basis. In early Christian communities the bishops, deans, and priests were elected by all the members of the congregation, and by this one measure the rulers and teachers of the several Churches, while amply availing themselves of the efficacious system of Roman administration, successfully avoided the mistake of estranging the bulk of their people from the interests of the Church. For, powerful as truth, and especially inspired truth, may be, in this practical and material world of ours, Truth will never make much headway, unless it is supported by adequate organization. And thus the reason why so many reformers of the first century failed was mainly a lack of proper organization.

This organization, however, the Christian teachers learned

from the system invented by the Romans. The Roman influence on Christianity is most strikingly illustrated by the very name of the adherents of the new creed. The Greek name of Christian is χριστιανός. Did it ever occur to you that this is no Greek form, or rather a late, and evidently Romanised form of a derivative? The New Testament was first written in Greek, and so were the Acts, where this word first occurs. But it was evidently framed after a Roman word, the ending ιανος being an un-Greek form. And in fact the immense practical force of the first Christian communities was mainly due to the force of institutions that were framed after the pattern of the Roman city-state. The central idea of this state was the absolute and uncompromising devotion of a limited number of free citizens to the tasks and duties of the state, without remuneration, without material profit. The moral elevation of these citizens in the heydays of Greek and Roman city-states was quite imposing. Their powers of self-control, modesty, unselfishness and devotion were taxed to the utmost. You remember what I had to say about the excessive scrupulousness that every Roman had to observe in the business affairs of his daily life. And thus the Roman commonwealth, as long as it remained unalloyed, was based externally on a city-state, internally on purely moral forces. This we see also in the Christian commonwealths; and still more.

The Christian commonwealth discarding, as it did, one of the factors, to wit the narrow limits of a city-state, had to intensify indefinitely the other factor, to wit the purely moral agencies on which it was built, and in addition to the common virtues of men, it created new virtues of women, declaring virginity a claim to sacredness, and total abstinence from the enjoyments of life to the character of Holiness. While, therefore, the Roman commonwealth was built on the moral excellence of a restricted number of men, the Christian commonwealth was erected on a more comprehensive moral excellence of both men and women. But the idea of erecting a state mainly on moral agencies was purely Graeco-Roman, and without this, the vital nerve of classical antiquity, Christian communities of the first three centuries could not have succeeded. The commonwealths of Asia and Africa were erected on foundations of an altogether different character. It is the distinctive sign and mark of classical antiquity that the pure emotional forces of men,— of a restricted number of men, it is true, were the ultimate safeguard and bulwark of the state. It is not incumbent upon me to trace the development of Christianity. But in my boundless admiration of classical antiquity, and in my profound conviction, that not the intellect but the emotions are the leading powers of men, I glory in the fact that Christianity, the saintliest and most important of all institutions of the last 1800 years, has taken both its external and internal organization from institutions that were established and upheld by the unimpaired and manly souls of Greece and Rome. Even in his hatred of heathen Rome, St. Augustine could not find a more fitting title for the commonwealth that he was struggling for, than a term that at once indicated the close relation between the Church of Christianity and the city-state of Rome, calling his work " *de Civitate Dei*," because he felt that the ultimate foundation of both was character and moral force. It is character and moral force that keep this world a going, and the brilliant sallies of the intellect could have established neither the city-state of Greece and Rome nor the glorious commonwealth of Christianity.

THE END.

INDEX.

H

Slavery, value of Roman Law of, 14 ; Roman and American, 41 ; a necessity to the Roman city-state, 80 ; origin of classical s., 80 ; not denounced by Aristotle or early Christian writers, 81.

Slaves, position of, 41-5 ; law relating to, 43 ; how they influenced formation of Roman law-concepts, *ib.*

Social war, purport of, 79.

Sparta, women of, 83.

Thalmud, similarity to *Corpus Juris*, 31.

Timocracy, Rome a, 38.

Types of Roman Law, the two, 41.

Universities, German, all founded by princes, 58 ; never founded by free cities, *ib.* ; why not established in Hungary, 62.

Usus, is it *jus* or *factum*, 45.

Ususfructus, is it *jus* or *factum*, 45.

Valse, Vienna, pillar of Austrian dynasty, 84.

Variations, 68.

Vico, on Roman Law, 66, 67.

Village Life and civilization, 76 ; none in America, *ib.*

Voting, system of Roman, 38.

Weisthuemer, 54.

Women, position of in Greece, 82 ; in Rome, 83 ; influence of in Graeco-Roman times, 84 ; importance of in Christian communities, 93.

Zumpt, on embezzlement, 22.

Printed by Parker and Co., Crown Yard, Oxford.

The One Religion.
Truth, Holiness, and Peace desired by the Nations, and Revealed by Jesus Christ. By the Right Rev. the LORD BISHOP OF SALISBURY. Second Edition. Crown 8vo., cloth, 7s. 6d.

The Administration of the Holy Spirit
IN THE BODY OF CHRIST. The Bampton Lectures for 1868. By the late LORD BISHOP OF SALISBURY. Third Edition. Crown 8vo., 7s. 6d.

An Explanation of the Thirty-Nine Articles.
By the late A. P. FORBES, D.C.L., Bishop of Brechin. With an Epistle Dedicatory to the Rev. E. B. PUSEY, D.D. New Edition, in one vol., Post 8vo., 12s.

A Short Explanation of the Nicene Creed,
For the Use of Persons beginning the Study of Theology. By the late A. P. FORBES, D.C.L., Bishop of Brechin. New Edition, Crown 8vo., cloth, 6s.

The Apostles' Creed.
The Greek Origin of the Apostles' Creed Illustrated by Ancient Documents and Recent Research. By Rev. JOHN BARON, D.D., F.S.A. 8vo., cloth, with Seven Illustrations, 10s. 6d.

The Sacraments.
RICHARD BAXTER ON THE SACRAMENTS: Holy Orders, Holy Baptism, Confirmation, Absolution, Holy Communion. 18mo., cloth, 1s.

The History of Confirmation.
By WILLIAM JACKSON, M.A., Queen's College, Oxford; Vicar of Heathfield, Sussex. Crown 8vo., cloth, 2s. 6d.

A Summary of the Ecclesiastical Courts Commission's Report:
And of Dr. STUBBS' Historical Reports; together with a Review of the Evidence before the Commission. By SPENCER L. HOLLAND, Barrister-at-Law. Post 8vo., cloth, 7s. 6d.

A History of Canon Law
In conjunction with other Branches of Jurisprudence: with Chapters on the Royal Supremacy and the Report of the Commission on Ecclesiastical Courts. By Rev. J. DODD, M.A., formerly Rector of Hampton Poyle, Oxon. 8vo., cloth, 7s. 6d.

The Philosophy of Church-Life,
Or The Church of Christ viewed as the Means whereby God manifests Himself to Mankind. By the late R. TUDOR, B.A., Vicar of Swallowcliffe, Wilts; Author of "The Decalogue viewed as the Christian's Law," &c. 2 vols., 8vo., cloth, 16s.
"A work which we do not hesitate to pronounce one of the most important contributions to scientific theology that has been made in our time."—*John Bull.*

On Eucharistical Adoration.

With Considerations suggested by a Pastoral Letter on the Doctrine of the Most Holy Eucharist. By the late Rev. JOHN KEBLE, M.A., Vicar of Hursley. 24mo., sewed, 2s.

The Catholic Doctrine of the Sacrifice and Participation of the Holy Eucharist.

By GEORGE TREVOR, M.A., D.D., Canon of York ; Rector of Beeford. Second Edition. 8vo., cloth, 10s. 6d.

S. Athanasius on the Incarnation, &c.

S. Patris Nostri S. Athanasii Archiepiscopi Alexandriæ de Incarnatione Verbi, ejusque Corporali ad nos Adventu. With an English Translation by the Rev. J. RIDGWAY, B.D., Hon. Canon of Ch. Ch. Fcap. 8vo., cloth, 5s.

De Fide et Symbolo :

Documenta quædam nec non Aliquorum SS. Patrum Tractatus. Edidit CAROLUS A. HEURTLEY, S.T.P., Dom. Margaretæ Prælector, et Ædis Christi Canonicus. Editio Quarta, Recognita et Aucta. Crown 8vo., cloth, 4s. 6d.

Translation of the above.
Cloth, 4s. 6d.

The Canons of the Church.

The Definitions of the Catholic Faith and Canons of Discipline of the First Four General Councils of the Universal Church. In Greek and English. Fcap. 8vo., cloth, 2s. 6d.

The English Canons.

The Constitutions and Canons Ecclesiastical of the Church of England, referred to their Original Sources, and Illustrated with Explanatory Notes, by MACKENZIE E. C. WALCOTT, B.D., F.S.A., Præcentor and Prebendary of Chichester. Fcap. 8vo., cloth, 2s. 6d.

Cur Deus Homo.

Or Why God was made Man ; by ST. ANSELM. Latin and English.

St. Cyril on the Mysteries.

The Five Lectures of St. Cyril on the Mysteries, and other Sacramental Treatises ; with Translations. Edited by the Rev. H. DE ROMESTIN, M.A., Great Maplestead, Essex. Fcap. 8vo., cloth. 3s.

S. Aurelius Augustinus,
EPISCOPUS HIPPONENSIS,

De Catechizandis Rudibus, de Fide Rerum quæ non videntur, de Utilitate Credendi. A New Edition with the Enchiridion. Fcap. 8vo., cloth, 3s. 6d.

Translation of the above.
Cloth, 3s. 6d.

Vincentius Lirinensis.

For the Antiquity and Universality of the Catholic Faith against the Profane Novelties of all Heretics. *Latin and English.* New Edition, Fcap. 8vo., 3s.

The Pastoral Rule of S. Gregory.

Sancti Gregorii Papæ Regulæ Pastoralis Liber, ad JOHANNEM, Episcopum Civitatis Ravennæ. With an English Translation. By the Rev. H. R. BRAMLEY, M.A., Fellow of Magdalen College, Oxford. Fcap. 8vo., cloth, 6s.

The Book of Ratramn.

The Priest and Monk of Corbey commonly called Bertram, on the Body and Blood of the Lord. (Latin and English.) Fcap. 8vo.

The Athanasian Creed.

A Critical History of the Athanasian Creed, by the Rev. DANIEL WATERLAND, D.D. Fcap. 8vo., cloth, 5s.

Διδαχὴ τῶν δώδεκα Ἀποστόλων.

The Teaching of the Twelve Apostles. The Greek Text with English Translation, Introduction, Notes, and Illustrative Passages. By the Rev. H. DE ROMESTIN, Incumbent of Freeland, and Rural Dean. Second Edition. Fcap. 8vo., cloth, 3s.

Studia Sacra :

Commentaries on the Introductory Verses of St. John's Gospel, and on a Portion of St. Paul's Epistle to the Romans; with an Analysis of St. Paul's Epistles, &c., by the late Rev. JOHN KEBLE, M.A. 8vo., cloth, 10s. 6d.

Discourses on Prophecy.

In which are considered its Structure, Use and Inspiration. By JOHN DAVISON, B.D. Sixth and Cheaper Edition. 8vo., cloth, 9s.

The Worship of the Old Covenant

CONSIDERED MORE ESPECIALLY IN RELATION TO THAT OF THE New. By the Rev. E. F. WILLIS, M.A., late Vice-Principal of Cuddesdon College. Post 8vo., cloth, 5s.

A Summary of the Evidences for the Bible.

By the Rev. T. S. ACKLAND, M.A., late Fellow of Clare Hall, Cambridge ; Incumbent of Pollington cum Balne, Yorkshire. 24mo., cloth, 3s.

A Plain Commentary on the Book of Psalms

(Prayer-book Version), chiefly grounded on the Fathers. For the Use of Families. 2 vols., Fcap. 8vo., cloth, 10s. 6d.

The Psalter and the Gospel.

The Life, Sufferings, and Triumph of our Blessed Lord, revealed in the Book of Psalms. Fcap. 8vo., cloth, 2s.

The Study of the New Testament :

Its Present Position, and some of its Problems. AN INAU-GURAL LECTURE delivered on Feb. 20th and 22nd, 1883. By W. SANDAY, M.A., D.D., Dean Ireland's Professor of the Exegesis of Holy Scripture. 64 pp. 8vo., in wrapper, 2s.

Sayings Ascribed to Our Lord

By the Fathers and other Primitive Writers, and Incidents in His Life narrated by them, otherwise than found in Scrip-ture. By JOHN THEODORE DODD, B.A., late Student of Christ Church, Oxford. Fcap. 8vo., cloth, 3s.

A Commentary on the Epistles and Gospels in the Book of Common Prayer.

Extracted from Writings of the Fathers of the Holy Catholic Church, anterior to the Division of the East and West. With an Introductory Notice by the DEAN OF ST. PAUL'S. 2 vols., Crown 8vo., cloth, 10s. 6d.

Catena Aurea.

A Commentary on the Four Gospels, collected out of the Works
of the Fathers by S. THOMAS AQUINAS. Uniform with the
Library of the Fathers. A Re-issue, complete in 6 vols.,
cloth, £2 2s.

A Plain Commentary on the Four Holy Gospels,

Intended chiefly for Devotional Reading. By the Very Rev.
J. W. BURGON, B.D., Dean of Chichester. New Edition.
4 vols., Fcap. 8vo., limp cloth, £1 1s.

The Last Twelve Verses of the Gospel according to S. Mark

Vindicated against Recent Critical Objectors and Established,
by the Very Rev. J. W. BURGON, B.D., Dean of Chichester.
With Facsimiles of Codex ℵ and Codex L. 8vo., cloth, 6s.

The Gospels from a Rabbinical Point of View,

Shewing the perfect Harmony of the Four Evangelists on the
subject of our Lord's Last Supper, and the Bearing of the
Laws and Customs of the Jews at the time of our Lord's
coming on the Language of the Gospels. By the late Rev. G.
W. PIERITZ, M.A. Crown 8vo., limp cloth, 3s.

Christianity as Taught by S. Paul.

By the late W. J. IRONS, D.D., of Queen's College, Oxford;
Prebendary of S. Paul's; being the BAMPTON LECTURES
for the Year 1870, with an Appendix of the CONTINUOUS
SENSE of S. Paul's Epistles; with Notes and Metalegomena,
8vo., with Map, Second Edition, with New Preface, cloth, 9s.

S. Paul's Epistles to the Ephesians and Philippians.

A Practical and Exegetical Commentary. Edited by the late
Rev. HENRY NEWLAND. 8vo., cloth, 7s. 6d.

The Explanation of the Apocalypse.

By VENERABLE BEDA, Translated by the Rev. EDW. MAR-
SHALL, M.A., F.S.A., formerly Fellow of Corpus Christi
College, Oxford. 180 pp. Fcap. 8vo., cloth, 3s. 6d.

A History of the Church,

From the Edict of Milan, A.D. 313, to the Council of Chalcedon, A.D. 451. By WILLIAM BRIGHT, D.D., Regius Professor of Ecclesiastical History, and Canon of Christ Church, Oxford. Second Edition. Post 8vo., 10s. 6d.

The Age of the Martyrs;

Or, The First Three Centuries of the Work of the Church of our Lord and Saviour Jesus Christ. By the late JOHN DAVID JENKINS, B.D., Fellow of Jesus College, Oxford; Canon of Pieter Maritzburg. Cr. 8vo., cl., reduced to 3s. 6d.

Eighteen Centuries of the Church in England.

By the Rev. A. H. HORE, M.A. Trinity College, Oxford. 712 pp. Demy 8vo., cloth, 15s.

The Ecclesiastical History of the First Three Centuries,

From the Crucifixion of Jesus Christ to the year 313. By the late Rev. Dr. BURTON. Fourth Edition. 8vo., cloth, 12s.

A Brief History of the Christian Church,

From the First Century to the Reformation. By the Rev. J. S. BARTLETT. Fcap. 8vo., cloth, 2s. 6d.

A History of the English Church,

From its Foundation to the Reign of Queen Mary. By MARY CHARLOTTE STAPLEY. Fourth Edition, revised, with a Recommendatory Notice by DEAN HOOK. Crown 8vo., cloth, 5s.

Bede's Ecclesiastical History of the English Nation.

A New Translation by the Rev. L. GIDLEY, M.A., Chaplain of St. Nicholas', Salisbury. Crown 8vo., cloth, 6s.

St. Paul in Britain;

Or, The Origin of British as opposed to Papal Christianity. By the Rev. R. W. MORGAN. Second Edition. Crown 8vo., cloth, 2s. 6d.

The Sufferings of the Clergy during the Great Rebellion.

By the Rev. JOHN WALKER, M.A., sometime of Exeter College, Oxford, and Rector of St. Mary Major, Exeter. Epitomised by the Author of "The Annals of England." Second Edition. Fcap. 8vo., cloth 2s. 6d.

Missale ad usum Insignis et Præclaræ Ecclesiæ Sarum.
Ed. F. H. DICKINSON, A.M. Complete in One Vol., 8vo., cl., 26s. Part II., 6s.; Part III., 10s. 6d.; and Part IV., 7s. 6d.; may still be had.

The First Prayer-Book of Edward VI. Compared
With the Successive Revisions of the Book of Common Prayer. Together with a Concordance and Index to the Rubrics in the several Editions. Second Edition. Crown 8vo., cloth, 12s.

An Introduction
TO THE HISTORY OF THE SUCCESSIVE REVI-sions of the Book of Common Prayer. By JAMES PARKER, Hon. M.A. Oxon. Crown 8vo., pp. xxxii., 532, cloth, 12s.

The Principles of Divine Service;
Or, An Inquiry concerning the True Manner of Understand-ing and Using the Order for Morning and Evening Prayer, and for the Administration of the Holy Communion in the English Church. By the late Ven. PHILIP FREEMAN, M.A., Archdeacon of Exeter, &c. 2 vols., 8vo., cloth, 16s.

A History of the Book of Common Prayer,
And other Authorized Books, from the Reformation; with an Account of the State of Religion in England from 1640 to 1660. By the Rev. THOMAS LATHBURY, M.A. Second Edition, with an Index. 8vo., cloth, 5s.

The Prayer-Book Calendar.
THE CALENDAR OF THE PRAYER-BOOK ILLUS-TRATED. (Comprising the first portion of the "Calendar of the Anglican Church," with additional Illustrations, an Appendix on Emblems, &c.) With 200 Engravings from Me-dieval Works of Art. Sixth Thousand. Fcap. 8vo., cl., 6s.

A CHEAP EDITION OF
The First Prayer-Book
As issued by the Authority of the Parliament of the Second Year of King Edward VI. 1549. Tenth Thousand. 24mo., limp cloth, price 1s.

Also,
The Second Prayer-Book of Edward VI.
Issued 1552. Fifth Thousand. 24mo., limp cloth, price 1s.

Ritual Conformity.
Interpretations of the Rubrics of the Prayer-Book, agreed upon by a Conference held at All Saints, Margaret-street, 1880—1881. Third Edition, 80 pp. Crown 8vo., in wrapper, 1s.

The Ornaments Rubrick,
ITS HISTORY AND MEANING. Fifth Thousand. 72 pp., Crown 8vo., 6d.

The Catechist's Manual;

By EDW. M. HOLMES, Rector of Marsh Gibbon, Bicester. With an Introduction by the late SAMUEL WILBERFORCE, LORD BP. OF WINCHESTER. 6th Thousand. Cr. 8vo., limp cl., 5*s*.

The Confirmation Class-book:

Notes for Lessons, with APPENDIX, containing Questions and Summaries for the Use of the Candidates. By EDWARD M. HOLMES, LL.B., Author of the "Catechist's Manual." Second Edition, Fcap. 8vo., limp cloth, 2*s. 6d*.

THE QUESTIONS, separate, 4 sets, in wrapper, 1*s*.
THE SUMMARIES, separate, 4 sets, in wrapper, 1*s*.

Catechetical Lessons on the Book of Common Prayer.

Illustrating the Prayer-book, from its Title-page to the end of the Collects, Epistles, and Gospels. Designed to aid the Clergy in Public Catechising. By the Rev. Dr. FRANCIS HESSEY, Incumbent of St. Barnabas, Kensington. Fcap. 8vo., cloth, 6*s*.

Catechising Notes on the Apostles' Creed;

The Ten Commandments; The Lord's Prayer; The Confirmation Service; The Forms of Prayer at Sea, &c. By A WORCESTERSHIRE CURATE. Crown 8vo., in wrapper, 1*s*.

The Church's Work in our Large Towns.

By GEORGE HUNTINGTON, M.A., Rector of Tenby, and Domestic Chaplain of the Rt. Hon. the Earl of Crawford and Balcarres. Second Edit., revised and enlarged. Cr. 8vo., cl. 3*s. 6d*.

Notes of Seven Years' Work in a Country Parish.

By R. F. WILSON, M.A., Prebendary of Sarum, and Examining Chaplain to the Bishop of Salisbury. Fcap. 8vo., cloth, 4*s*.

A Manual of Pastoral Visitation,

Intended for the Use of the Clergy in their Visitation of the Sick and Afflicted. By A PARISH PRIEST. Dedicated, by permission, to His Grace the Archbishop of Dublin. Second Edition, Crown 8vo., limp cloth, 3*s. 6d*. ; roan, 4*s*.

The Cure of Souls.

By the Rev. G. ARDEN, M.A., Rector of Winterborne-Came, and Author of "Breviates from Holy Scripture," &c. Fcap. 8vo., cloth, 2*s. 6d*.

Questions on the Collects, Epistles, and Gospels,

Throughout the Year. Edited by the Rev. T. L. CLAUGHTON, Vicar of Kidderminster. For the Use of Teachers in Sunday Schools. Fifth Edition, 18mo., cl. In two Parts, *each* 2*s. 6d*.

Addresses to the Candidates for Ordination on the Questions in the Ordination Service.

By the late SAMUEL WILBERFORCE, LORD BISHOP OF WINCHESTER. Fifth Thousand. Crown 8vo., cloth, 6*s*.

Tracts for the Christian Seasons.

FIRST SERIES. Edited by JOHN ARMSTRONG, D.D., late Lord Bishop of Grahamstown. 4 vols. complete, Fcap. 8vo., cloth, 12*s.*

SECOND SERIES. Edited by JOHN ARMSTRONG, D.D., late Lord Bishop of Grahamstown. 4 vols. complete, Fcap. 8vo., cloth, 10*s.*

THIRD SERIES. Edited by JAMES RUSSELL WOODFORD, D.D., late Lord Bishop of Ely. 4 vols., Fcap. 8vo., cloth, 14*s.*

Faber's Stories from the Old Testament.

With Four Illustrations. New Edition. Square Crown 8vo., cloth, 4*s.*

Holy Order.

A CATECHISM. By CHARLES S. GRUEBER, Vicar of S. James, Hambridge, Diocese of Bath and Wells. 220 pp. 24mo., in wrapper, 3*s.*

By the same Author.

The Church of England the Ancient Church of the Land.

Its Property. Disestablishment and Disendowment. Fate of Sacrilege. Work and Progress of the Church, &c., &c. A CATECHISM. Second Edition, 24mo., in wrapper, 1*s.*

A Catechism on the Kingdom of God:

For the Use of the Children of the Kingdom in Sunday and Day Schools. Second Edition, 70 pp. 24mo., cloth, 1*s.*; in stiff wrapper, 6*d.*

"Is Christ Divided?"

On Unity in Religion, and the Sin and Scandal of Schism, That is to say, of Division, Disunion, Separation, among Christians. A CATECHISM. 8vo., in wrapper, 1*s.*

The Catechism of the Church of England

Commented upon, and Illustrated from the Holy Scriptures and the Book of Common Prayer, with Appendices on Confirmation, &c., &c. 24mo., limp cloth, 1*s.*; cloth boards, 1*s.* 6*d.*

For a Series of Parochial Books and Tracts published by Messrs. Parker, see the Parochial Catalogue.

𝔒𝔵𝔣𝔬𝔯𝔡 𝔈𝔡𝔦𝔱𝔦𝔬𝔫𝔰 𝔬𝔣 𝔇𝔢𝔟𝔬𝔱𝔦𝔬𝔫𝔞𝔩 𝔚𝔬𝔯𝔨𝔰.

Fcap. 8vo., chiefly printed in Red and Black, on Toned Paper.

Andrewes' Devotions.
DEVOTIONS. By the Right Rev. LANCELOT ANDREWES. Translated from the Greek and Latin, and arranged anew. Cloth, 5s.

The Imitation of Christ.
FOUR BOOKS. By THOMAS A KEMPIS. A new Edition, revised. Cloth, 4s.
Pocket Edition. 32mo., cloth, 1s.; bound, 1s. 6d.

Laud's Devotions.
THE PRIVATE DEVOTIONS of Dr. WILLIAM LAUD, Archbishop of Canterbury, and Martyr. Antique cloth, 5s.

Spinckes' Devotions.
TRUE CHURCH OF ENGLAND MAN'S COMPANION IN THE CLOSET. By NATHANIEL SPINCKES. Floriated borders, antique cloth, 4s.

Sutton's Meditations.
GODLY MEDITATIONS UPON THE MOST HOLY SACRAMENT OF THE LORD'S SUPPER. By CHRISTOPHER SUTTON, D.D., late Prebend of Westminster. A new Edition. Antique cloth, 5s.

Devout Communicant.
THE DEVOUT COMMUNICANT, exemplified in his Behaviour before, at, and after the Sacrament of the Lord's Supper: Practically suited to all the Parts of that Solemn Ordinance. 7th Edition, revised. Edited by Rev. G. MOULTRIE. Fcap. 8vo., toned paper, red lines, ant. cloth, 4s.

Taylor's Holy Living.
THE RULE AND EXERCISES OF HOLY LIVING. By BISHOP JEREMY TAYLOR. Antique cloth, 4s.
Pocket Edition. 32mo., cloth, 1s.; bound, 1s. 6d.

Taylor's Holy Dying.
THE RULE AND EXERCISES OF HOLY DYING. By BISHOP JEREMY TAYLOR. Ant. cloth, 4s.
Pocket Edition. 32mo., cloth, 1s.; bound, 1s. 6d.

Taylor's Golden Grove.
THE GOLDEN GROVE: A Choice Manual, containing what is to be Believed, Practised, and Desired or Prayed for. By BISHOP JEREMY TAYLOR. Antique cloth, 3s. 6d.

Wilson's Sacra Privata.
SACRA PRIVATA. The Private Meditations, Devotions, and Prayers of the Right Rev. T. WILSON, D.D., Lord Bishop of Sodor and Man. Now first Printed entire, from the Original Manuscripts. Antique cloth, 4s.

ΕΙΚΩΝ ΒΑΣΙΛΙΚΗ.
THE PORTRAITURE OF HIS SACRED MAJESTY KING CHARLES I. in his Solitudes and Sufferings. New Edition, with an Historical Preface by C. M. PHILLIMORE. Cloth, 5s.

Ancient Collects.
ANCIENT COLLECTS AND OTHER PRAYERS, Selected for Devotional Use from various Rituals, with an Appendix on the Collects in the Prayer-book. By WILLIAM BRIGHT, D.D. Fourth Edition. Antique cloth, 5s.

EUCHARISTICA:

Meditations and Prayers on the Most Holy Eucharist, from Old English Divines. With an Introduction by SAMUEL, LORD BISHOP OF OXFORD. A New Edition, revised by the Rev. H. E. CLAYTON, Vicar of S. Mary Magdalene, Oxford. In Red and Black, 32mo., cloth, 2s. 6d.—Cheap Edition, 1s.

DAILY STEPS TOWARDS HEAVEN ;

Or, PRACTICAL THOUGHTS on the GOSPEL HISTORY, for Every Day in the Year. Fiftieth Thousand. 32mo., roan, 2s. 6d. ; morocco, 5s.

LARGE-TYPE EDITION. Crown 8vo., cloth antique, 5s.

THE HOURS:

Being Prayers for the Third, Sixth, and Ninth Hours ; with a Preface and Heads of Devotion for the Day. Seventh Edition. 32mo., 1s.

PRIVATE PRAYERS FOR A WEEK.

Compiled by WILLIAM BRIGHT, D.D., Canon of Christ Church, Oxford. 96 pp. Fcap. 8vo., limp cloth, 1s. 6d.

By the same Author.

FAMILY PRAYERS FOR A WEEK.

Fcap. 8vo., cloth, 1s.

STRAY THOUGHTS:

For Every Day in the Year. Collected and Arranged by E. L. 32mo., cloth gilt, red edges, 1s.

OUTLINES OF INSTRUCTIONS

Or Meditations for the Church's Seasons. By the late JOHN KEBLE, M.A. Edited, with a Preface, by the late R. F. WILSON, M.A. Second Edition. Crown 8vo., cloth, toned paper, 5s.

SPIRITUAL COUNSEL, ETC.

By the late Rev. J. KEBLE, M.A. Edited by the late R. F. WILSON, M.A. Fifth Edition. Post 8vo., cloth, 3s. 6d.

MEDITATIONS FOR THE FORTY DAYS OF LENT.

By the Author of "Charles Lowder." With a Prefatory Notice by the ARCHBISHOP OF DUBLIN, 18mo., cloth, 2s. 6d.

OF THE IMITATION OF CHRIST.

Four Books. By THOMAS A KEMPIS. Small 4to., printed on thick toned paper, with red border-lines, &c. Cloth, 12s.

PRAYERS FOR MARRIED PERSONS.

From Various Sources, chiefly from the Ancient Liturgies. Selected by C. WARD, M.A. Third Edition, Revised. 24mo., cloth, 4s. 6d. ; Cheap Edition, 2s. 6d.

FOR THE LORD'S SUPPER.

DEVOTIONS BEFORE AND AFTER HOLY COMMUNION. With Preface by J. KEBLE. Sixth Edition. 32mo., cloth, 2s.

With the Office, cloth, 2s. 6d.

The late Osborne Gordon.

OSBORNE GORDON. A Memoir : with a Selection of his Writings. Edited by Geo. Marshall, M.A., Rector of Milton, Berks, &c. With Medallion Portrait, 8vo., cloth, 10s. 6d.

Dr. Preston.

THE LIFE OF THE RENOWNED DR. PRESTON. Writ by his Pupil, Master Thomas Ball, D.D., Minister of Northampton in the year 1628. Edited by E. W. Harcourt, Esq., M.P. Crown 8vo., cloth, 4s.

Rev. John Keble.

A MEMOIR OF THE REV. JOHN KEBLE, M.A., late Vicar of Hursley. By the Right Hon. Sir J. T. Coleridge, D.C.L. Fifth Edition. Post 8vo., cloth, 6s.

OCCASIONAL PAPERS AND REVIEWS, on Sir Walter Scott, Poetry, and Sacred Poetry. By the late Rev. John Keble. Author of "The Christian Year." Demy 8vo., cloth extra, 12s.

Archdeacon Denison.

NOTES OF MY LIFE, 1805—1878. By George Anthony Denison, Vicar of East Brent, 1845 : Archdeacon of Taunton, 1851. Third Edition, 8vo., cloth, 12s.

Bishop Herbert de Losinga.

THE FOUNDER OF NORWICH CATHEDRAL. The LIFE, LETTERS, and SERMONS of BISHOP HERBERT DE LOSINGA (b. circ. a.d. 1050, d. 1119). By Edward Meyrick Goulburn, D.D., Dean of Norwich, and Henry Symonds, M.A. 2 vols., 8vo., cloth, 30s.

John Armstrong.

LIFE OF JOHN ARMSTRONG, D.D., late Lord Bishop of Grahamstown. By the Rev. T. T. Carter, M.A., Rector of Clewer. Third Edition. Fcap. 8vo., with Portrait, cloth, 7s. 6d.

Bishop Wilson.

THE LIFE OF THE RIGHT REVEREND FATHER IN GOD, THOMAS WILSON, D.D., Lord Bishop of Sodor and Man. By the late Rev. John Keble, M.A., Vicar of Hursley. 2 vols., 8vo., cloth, £1 1s.

THE SAINTLY LIFE OF MRS. MARGARET GODOLPHIN. 16mo., 1s.

FOOTPRINTS ON THE SANDS OF TIME. Biographies for Young People. Fcap., limp cloth, 2s. 6d.

THE AUTHORIZED EDITIONS OF

THE CHRISTIAN YEAR,

With the Author's latest Corrections and Additions.

NOTICE.—Messrs. PARKER are the sole Publishers of the Editions of the "Christian Year" issued with the sanction and under the direction of the Author's representatives. All Editions without their imprint are unauthorized.

Handsomely printed on toned paper. SMALL 4to. EDITION.	*s.*	*d.*		32mo. EDITION.		*s.*	*d.*
				Cloth, limp		1	0
Cloth extra . . .	10	6		Cloth boards, gilt edges .		1	6
				48mo. EDITION.			
DEMY 8vo. EDITION. Cloth	6	0		Cloth, limp		0	6
FCAP. 8vo. EDITION. Cloth	3	6		Roan		1	6
				FACSIMILE OF THE 1ST EDI-			
24mo. EDIT. With red lines, cl.	2	6		TION. 2 vols., 12mo., boards		7	6

The above Editions are kept in a variety of bindings.

By the same Author.

LYRA INNOCENTIUM. Thoughts in Verse on Christian Children. *Thirteenth Edition.* Fcap. 8vo., cloth, 5*s.*
————— 48mo. edition, limp cloth, 6*d.* ; cloth boards, 1*s.*
MISCELLANEOUS POEMS by the Rev. JOHN KEBLE, M.A., Vicar of Hursley. *Third Edition.* Fcap. cloth, 6*s.*
THE PSALTER OR PSALMS OF DAVID : In English Verse. *Fourth Edition.* Fcap., cloth, 6*s.*

The above may also be had in various bindings.

By the late Rev. ISAAC WILLIAMS.

THE CATHEDRAL ; or, The Catholic and Apostolic Church in England. Fcap. 8vo., cloth, 5*s.*; 32mo., cloth, 2*s.* 6*d.*
THE BAPTISTERY ; or, The Way of Eternal Life. Fcap. 8vo., cloth, 7*s.* 6*d.* (with the Plates) ; 32mo., cloth, 2*s.* 6*d.*
HYMNS translated from the PARISIAN BREVIARY. 32mo., cloth, 2*s.* 6*d.*
THE CHRISTIAN SCHOLAR. Fcap. 8vo., cloth, 5*s.* ; 32mo., cloth, 2*s.* 6*d.*
THOUGHTS IN PAST YEARS. 32mo., cloth, 2*s.* 6*d.*
THE SEVEN DAYS ; or, The Old and New Creation. Fcap. 8vo., cloth, 3*s.* 6*d.*

CHRISTIAN BALLADS AND POEMS.

By ARTHUR CLEVELAND COXE, D.D., Bishop of Western New York. A New Edition, printed in Red and Black, Fcap. 8vo., cloth, 2*s.* 6*d.*—Cheap Edition, 1*s.*

The POEMS of GEORGE HERBERT.

THE TEMPLE. Sacred Poems and Private Ejaculations. A New Edition, in Red and Black 24mo., cloth, 2*s.* 6*d.*—Cheap Edition, 1*s.*

THE ARCHBISHOP OF CANTERBURY.

SINGLEHEART. By Dr. EDWARD WHITE BENSON, Archbishop of Canterbury, late Bishop of Truro, &c. ADVENT SERMONS, 1876, preached in Lincoln Cathedral. Second Edition. Crown 8vo., cloth, 2s. 6d.

THE BISHOP OF SALISBURY.

UNIVERSITY SERMONS ON GOSPEL SUBJECTS. By the Right Rev. the LORD BISHOP OF SALISBURY. Fcap. 8vo., cl., 2s. 6d.

THE LATE BISHOP OF SALISBURY.

SERMONS ON THE BEATITUDES, with others mostly preached before the University of Oxford ; to which is added a Preface relating to the volume of "Essays and Reviews." New Edition. Crown 8vo., cloth, 7s. 6d.

THE BISHOP OF NEWCASTLE.

THE AWAKING SOUL. As sketched in the 130th Psalm. Addresses delivered at St. Peter's, Eaton-square, on the Tuesdays in Lent, 1877, by E. R. WILBERFORCE, M.A. [Rt. Rev. the Lord Bp. of Newcastle]. Crown 8vo., limp cloth, 2s. 6d.

THE BISHOP OF BARBADOS.

SERMONS PREACHED ON SPECIAL OCCASIONS. By JOHN MITCHINSON, D.D., late Bishop of Barbados. Crown 8vo., cloth, 5s.

VERY REV. THE DEAN OF CHICHESTER.

SHORT SERMONS FOR FAMILY READING, following the Course of the Christian Seasons. By Very Rev. J. W. BURGON, B.D., Dean of Chichester. First Series. 2 vols., Fcap. 8vo., cloth, 8s.
—— SECOND SERIES. 2 vols., Fcap. 8vo., cloth, 8s.

VERY REV. THE DEAN OF ROCHESTER.

HINTS TO PREACHERS, ILLUSTRATED BY SERMONS AND ADDRESSES. By S. REYNOLDS HOLE, Dean of Rochester. Second Edition. Post 8vo., cloth, 6s.

REV. J. KEBLE.

SERMONS, OCCASIONAL AND PAROCHIAL. By the late Rev. JOHN KEBLE, M.A., Vicar of Hursley. 8vo., cloth, 12s.

THE REV. CANON PAGET.

THE REDEMPTION OF WORK. ADDRESSES spoken in St. Paul's Cathedral, by FRANCIS PAGET, M.A., Senior Student of Christ Church, Oxford. 52 pp. Fcap. 8vo., cloth, 2s.

CONCERNING SPIRITUAL GIFTS. Three Addresses to Candidates for Holy Orders in the Diocese of Ely. With a Sermon. By FRANCIS PAGET, M.A., Senior Student of Christ Church, Oxford. Fcap. 8vo., cloth, 2s. 6d.

𝔚orks of the 𝔖tandard 𝔈nglish 𝔇iuines,

PUBLISHED IN THE LIBRARY OF ANGLO-CATHOLIC THEOLOGY.

Andrewes' (Bp.) Complete Works. 11 vols., 8vo., £3 7s.
THE SERMONS. (Separate.) 5 vols., £1 15s.

Beveridge's (Bp.) Complete Works. 12 vols., 8vo., £4 4s.
THE ENGLISH THEOLOGICAL WORKS. 10 vols., £3 10s.

Bramhall's (Abp.) Works, with Life and Letters, &c.
5 vols., 8vo., £1 15s.

Bull's (Bp.) Harmony on Justification. 2 vols., 8vo., 10s.
———————— Defence of the Nicene Creed. 2 vols., 10s.
———————— Judgment of the Catholic Church. 5s.

Cosin's (Bp.) Works Complete. 5 vols., 8vo., £1 10s.

Crakanthorp's Defensio Ecclesiæ Anglicanæ. 8vo., 7s.

Frank's Sermons. 2 vols., 8vo., 10s.

Forbes' Considerationes Modestæ. 2 vols., 8vo., 12s.

Gunning's Paschal, or Lent Fast. 8vo., 6s.

Hammond's Practical Catechism. 8vo., 5s.
———————— Miscellaneous Theological Works. 5s.
———————— Thirty-one Sermons. 2 Parts. 10s.

Hickes's Two Treatises on the Christian Priesthood.
3 vols., 8vo., 15s.

Johnson's (John) Theological Works. 2 vols., 8vo., 10s.
———————— English Canons. 2 vols., 12s.

Laud's (Abp.) Complete Works. 7 vols., (9 Parts,) 8vo.,
£2 17s.

L'Estrange's Alliance of Divine Offices. 8vo., 6s.

Marshall's Penitential Discipline. 8vo., 4s.

Nicholson's (Bp.) Exposition of the Catechism. (This
volume cannot be sold separate from the complete set.)

Overall's (Bp.) Convocation-book of 1606. 8vo., 5s.

Pearson's (Bp.) Vindiciæ Epistolarum S. Ignatii.
2 vols., 8vo., 10s.

Thorndike's (Herbert) Theological Works Complete.
6 vols., (10 Parts,) 8vo., £2 10s.

Wilson's (Bp.) Works Complete. With Life, by Rev.
J. KEBLE. 7 vols., (8 Parts,) 8vo., £3 3s.

⁎ *The* 81 *Vols. in* 88, *for* £15 15s. *net.*

HISTORICAL TALES,

Illustrating the Chief Events in Ecclesiastical History British and Foreign, &c.

Fcap. 8vo., 1s. each Tale, or 3s. 6d. each Volume in cloth.

ENGLAND. Vol. I.

1.—THE CAVE IN THE HILLS; or, Cæcilius Viriathus.
5.—WILD SCENES AMONGST THE CELTS.
7.—THE RIVALS: A Tale of the Anglo-Saxon Church.
10.—THE BLACK DANES.
14.—THE ALLELUIA BATTLE; or, Pelagianism in Britain.

ENGLAND. Vol. II.

16.—ALICE OF FOBBING; or, The Times of Jack Straw and Wat Tyler.
18.—AUBREY DE L'ORNE; or, The Times of St. Anselm.
21.— THE FORSAKEN; or, The Times of St. Dunstan.
24.—WALTER THE ARMOURER; or, The Interdict.
27.—AGNES MARTIN; or, The Fall of Cardinal Wolsey.

AMERICA AND OUR COLONIES.

3.—THE CHIEF'S DAUGHTER; or, The Settlers in Virginia.
8.—THE CONVERT OF MASSACHUSETTS.
20.—WOLFINGHAM; or, The Convict Settler of Jervis Bay.
25.—THE CATECHUMENS OF THE COROMANDEL COAST.
28.—ROSE AND MINNIE; or, The Loyalist: A Tale of Canada in 1837.

FRANCE AND SPAIN.

2.—THE EXILES OF THE CEBENNA; a Journal written during the Decian Persecution.
22.—THE DOVE OF TABENNA; and THE RESCUE.
23.—LARACHE: A Tale of the Portuguese Church in the Sixteenth Century.
29.—DORES DE GUALDIM: A Tale of the Portuguese Revolution.

EASTERN AND NORTHERN EUROPE.

6.—THE LAZAR-HOUSE OF LEROS: a Tale of the Eastern Church
11.—THE CONVERSION OF ST. VLAdimir; or, The Martyrs of Kief.
13.—THE CROSS IN SWEDEN; or,The Days of King Ingi the Good
17.—THE NORTHERN LIGHT: A Tale of Iceland and Greenland
26.—THE DAUGHTERS OF POLA a Tale of the Great Tenth Persecution.

ASIA AND AFRICA.

4.—THE LILY OF TIFLIS: a Sketch from Georgian Church History.
9.—THE QUAY OF THE DIOSCURI: a Tale of Nicene Times.
12.—THE SEA-TIGERS: A Tale of Mediæval Nestorianism.
15.—THE BRIDE OF RAMCUTTAH: A Tale of the Jewish Missions.
19.—LUCIA'S MARRIAGE; or, The Lions of Wady-Araba.

The late Dr. Elvey's Psalter.

Just published, 16mo.. cloth, 1s.; by Post, 1s. 2d.
A CHEAP EDITION (being the 20th) of
THE PSALTER; or, Canticles and Psalms of David.
Pointed for Chanting on a New Principle. With Explanations and Directions. By the late STEPHEN ELVEY, Mus. Doc., Organist of New and St. John's Colleges, and Organist and Choragus to the University of Oxford. With a Memorandum on the Pointing of the *Gloria Patri*, by Sir G. J. ELVEY.

Also,

II. FCAP. 8vo. EDITION (the 21st), limp cloth, 2s. 6d. With PROPER PSALMS. 3s.
III. LARGE TYPE EDITION for ORGAN (the 18th). Demy 8vo., cloth, 5s.
THE PROPER PSALMS separately. Fcap. 8vo., sewed, 6d.
THE CANTICLES separately (18th Edition). Fcap. 8vo., 3d.
The Psalter is used at St. George's Chapel, Windsor, and at many Cathedrals.

OXFORD AND LONDON: PARKER AND CO.

www.ingramcontent.com/pod-product-compliance
Lightning Source LLC
Chambersburg PA
CBHW030622270326
41927CB00007B/1278